Cryptocurrency
Investing

THE ULTIMATE GUIDE TO
CRYPTOCURRENCY INVESTING:
MAXIMIZING PROFITS IN
THE DIGITAL ASSET MARKET

Owen Harrington

TABLE OF CONTENTS

INTRODUCTION

Welcome to "Cryptocurrency Investing: The Ultimate Guide to Cryptocurrency Investing - Maximizing Profits in the Digital Asset Market." In today's digital age, cryptocurrencies have emerged as a revolutionary financial asset class, captivating the attention of investors worldwide. This e-book aims to provide comprehensive insights into cryptocurrency investing, equipping you with the knowledge and tools necessary to navigate this dynamic and potentially lucrative market.

Cryptocurrencies like Bitcoin and Ethereum have significantly increased in popularity in recent years, disrupting traditional financial systems and offering exciting investment opportunities. However, with this burgeoning market comes a range of complexities and risks that must be understood and managed effectively. That's where this guide comes in.

In the following pages, we will explore the fundamental concepts of cryptocurrencies, delve into the intricacies of blockchain technology, and discuss the various factors that influence the value and potential of digital assets. Whether you are a seasoned investor looking to expand your portfolio or a beginner eager to embark on your cryptocurrency investing journey, this guide will be your trusted companion.

We will begin by laying the groundwork, providing a solid understanding of cryptocurrencies and their evolution. You will learn about the different types of cryptocurrencies and the underlying technology that powers them - blockchain. Armed with this knowledge, we will guide you through the essential steps of getting started, including choosing a reputable cryptocurrency exchange, creating a digital wallet, and adopting robust security measures to safeguard your investments.

Investing in cryptocurrencies involves a blend of art and science. In this e-book, we will explore fundamental and technical analysis techniques to help you evaluate cryptocurrencies and make informed investment decisions. You will gain insights into conducting thorough research, analyzing project teams, assessing market demand, and understanding various tools and indicators used in technical analysis.

Building a well-defined investment strategy is crucial for long-term success. We will guide you through setting investment goals, managing risk, and diversifying your portfolio. Additionally, we will explore strategies for maximizing profits, including active trading techniques, participation in initial coin offerings (ICOs) and security token offerings (STOs), and leveraging passive income opportunities like yield farming and staking.

The world of cryptocurrency investing has its challenges. We will address common obstacles investors face, such as managing emotions, dealing with market volatility, and staying informed amidst rapid changes. By understanding these challenges and implementing appropriate strategies, you can navigate the cryptocurrency market with greater confidence and resilience.

Finally, we will discuss the future of cryptocurrency investing, examining emerging trends, potential regulatory changes, and the impact of cutting-edge technologies. By focusing on the horizon, you will be well-equipped to adapt to the evolving landscape and seize opportunities.

As you embark on your cryptocurrency investing journey, remember that knowledge and informed decision-making are essential. This e-book aims to empower you with the necessary tools, strategies, and insights to make the most of your investments in the digital asset market. So, without further ado, let's dive into the exciting world of cryptocurrency investing and unlock the potential for maximizing profits in this rapidly evolving landscape.

CHAPTER I

Understanding Cryptocurrencies

Definition and characteristics of cryptocurrencies

Cryptocurrencies have emerged as a revolutionary form of digital currency that has disrupted traditional financial systems and captured the imagination of investors worldwide. In this section, we will explore the definition and characteristics of cryptocurrencies, shedding light on their underlying technology, decentralization, security, transparency, and potential impact on the global economy. By understanding these fundamental aspects, we can better appreciate the unique qualities that make cryptocurrencies a compelling investment option and a catalyst for financial innovation.

Cryptocurrencies, commonly referred to as virtual or digital currency, can be defined as digital or virtual representations of value that utilize cryptographic methods for controlling the generation of new units and for securing transactions. Unlike traditional fiat currencies issued by central banks, cryptocurrencies operate on decentralized networks known as blockchains, which are public ledgers of all transactions. The decentralized nature of cryptocurrencies and their reliance on cryptographic principles provide several distinct advantages over traditional forms of money.

One of the defining features of cryptocurrencies is their strong emphasis on cryptographic security. Employing cryptographic methods ensures the confidentiality of financial transactions, maintains control over generating new units, and validates the system's overall integrity. Public-key cryptography, which involves using public and private keys, ensures transaction authenticity, integrity, and confidentiality. Cryptographic algorithms ensure that transactions are securely verified and recorded on the blockchain, protecting the privacy and security of participants.

Another critical characteristic of cryptocurrencies is their decentralized nature. Central authorities, such as governments or banks typically control traditional financial systems. However, because cryptocurrencies are built on decentralized networks, no single organization or group has complete control over the currency. This decentralized structure provides greater autonomy, transparency, and resilience to censorship and manipulation. Decentralization allows cryptocurrencies to operate independently of any central authority, ensuring that transactions are not subject to interference or control from third parties.

Cryptocurrencies rely on blockchain technology, a distributed ledger system that ensures the integrity and transparency of transactions. A blockchain is made up of a series of interconnected blocks, each of which has a list of verified transactions. Since these blocks are connected by means of cryptographic techniques, it is very difficult to change or tamper with the data that has been stored. Because of the extreme security and immutability offered by this technology, cryptocurrencies are resistant to fraud and hacker efforts. The decentralized and open nature of blockchain technology supports the potential for new business models and applications outside of traditional finance while enhancing participant trust.

Since a maximum number of units may ever be produced, many cryptocurrencies have a limited supply. For example, Bitcoin has a predetermined supply cap of 21 million coins. This limited supply introduces scarcity and can contribute to the potential value appreciation of cryptocurrencies over time. Additionally, some cryptocurrencies employ a process called mining, where participants use computational power to solve complex mathematical problems, validate transactions, and secure the network. Miners are rewarded with new units of cryptocurrency as an incentive for their efforts.

This process secures the network and regulates the creation and distribution of new units, adding fairness and economic incentive to the ecosystem.

The decentralized nature of cryptocurrencies allows for greater autonomy and freedom in financial transactions. Cryptocurrencies enable peer-to-peer transactions that are faster, more cost-effective, and less reliant on traditional financial institutions by eliminating the need for intermediaries, such as banks or payment processors. This decentralization also reduces the risk of censorship and provides access to financial services for individuals and businesses in underserved regions or those excluded from traditional banking systems. The decentralized nature of cryptocurrencies fosters financial inclusion and promotes economic empowerment.

Cryptocurrencies enable direct transactions between individuals or entities without the need for intermediaries. The peer-to-peer nature of cryptocurrency transactions allows for incredible speed and efficiency, as transactions can be settled directly between parties without delays associated with traditional financial systems. This aspect of cryptocurrencies enhances the potential for frictionless global transactions, enabling individuals and businesses to transact across borders easily.

To make transactions easier, traditional financial systems sometimes depend on the involvement of middlemen like banks or payment processors. These intermediaries introduce additional costs, delays, and potential points of failure in the system. With cryptocurrencies, the need for intermediaries is eliminated, resulting in faster and more cost-effective transactions. Removing intermediaries also reduces the risk of censorship, as transactions cannot be blocked or frozen by a central authority.

Decentralized networks, such as blockchains, promote trust and transparency in cryptocurrency transactions. All transactions are recorded on the blockchain, which serves as a public ledger accessible to anyone. This transparency allows participants to independently verify the integrity of transactions, ensuring that the system operates with integrity. It reduces the need for trust in third parties because it is possible to monitor the movement of money and confirm that transactions are genuine.

Blockchain technology forms the backbone of cryptocurrencies, enabling secure and transparent transactions. The unique characteristics of blockchain technology contribute to the trustworthiness and efficiency of cryptocurrencies, opening up new possibilities for applications beyond digital currency.

The decentralized nature of blockchain technology ensures that once a transaction is recorded on the blockchain, it becomes part of an immutable and permanent record. This immutability prevents tampering or alteration of transaction history, providing a high level of security and trust. The immutability of the blockchain makes it extremely difficult for bad actors to manipulate or alter transaction data, enhancing the system's integrity.

Blockchain technology employs a distributed consensus mechanism to validate and agree upon the ledger's state. Consensus methods, like

Proof of Work (PoW) and Proof of Stake (PoS), guarantee that network users agree on the legitimacy of transactions and the order in which they should be recorded. This distributed consensus mechanism prevents double-spending and ensures the ledger's consistency across all network nodes. The use of distributed consensus enhances the security and reliability of cryptocurrencies.

Blockchain technology is used to establish and carry out smart contracts, which are basically self-executing contracts with the conditions of the agreement explicitly written in code. Because they automatically carry out predetermined requirements when specific conditions are met, smart contracts do away with the necessity for middlemen in contractual agreements. Decentralized applications (DApps) can be developed on blockchain platforms like Ethereum that make use of the transparency, security, and decentralized characteristics of the technology. Smart contracts and DApps open up new possibilities for innovative business models and applications in various sectors beyond finance.

Cryptocurrencies rely on advanced cryptographic techniques to ensure the security and integrity of transactions. These cryptographic principles provide privacy, authenticity, and confidentiality, protecting the participants and their assets.

Public-key cryptography is a fundamental cryptographic technique used in cryptocurrencies. A public key and a private key, a pair of cryptographic keys, are used. As the name suggests, the public key is publicly shared and used to encrypt data or verify digital signatures. The private key, on the other hand, is kept secret and used to decrypt data or create digital signatures. This asymmetric encryption scheme provides secure communication between participants and verifies the authenticity of transactions.

Digital signatures are a crucial component of cryptocurrency transactions. A digital signature is created using the sender's private key and serves as proof of authenticity and integrity. By attaching a digital signature to a transaction, the sender can prove that they are the rightful owner of the cryptocurrency and that the transaction has not been tampered with. Digital signatures ensure that transactions are secure and verifiable, protecting against fraud and unauthorized access.

Cryptocurrencies rely on cryptographic hash functions to maintain the integrity of transactions and ensure data consistency. A hash function creates a unique fixed-length output from an input (like a transaction). Any alteration to the input yields an entirely different output. By including the previous block's hash in each block, blockchain technology creates a chain of blocks that are intrinsically linked and resistant to tampering. Hash functions provide a high level of security and make it computationally infeasible to alter transaction data.

While cryptocurrencies offer a certain level of privacy, they also promote transparency in transactional activities. The blockchain, being a public ledger, allows anyone to view and verify transactions. This transparency fosters trust within the system, as users can independently verify the integrity of transactions and track the flow of funds. However, it is worth noting that cryptocurrencies often provide varying levels of privacy, with some offering enhanced privacy features to protect user identities.

Transactions conducted using cryptocurrencies are recorded on the blockchain, which is a public ledger accessible to anyone. The public nature of the ledger allows anyone to view and verify transactions, ensuring that the system operates transparently. This transparency enhances trust among participants, as they can independently validate transaction details and monitor the movement of funds.

While transactions on the blockchain are transparent, the participants' identities are often pseudonymous. Participants are represented by cryptographic addresses rather than their real-world identities. This pseudonymity provides a certain level of privacy and protects users' identities. However, it is important to note that pseudonymity does not necessarily provide complete anonymity, as transactional patterns and other metadata can still reveal information about users.

Recognizing the need for enhanced privacy, some cryptocurrencies have introduced privacy-focused features and protocols. For instance, to increase privacy and anonymity, cryptocurrencies like Monero and Zcash use advanced cryptographic techniques like ring signatures and zero-knowledge proofs. These privacy-focused cryptocurrencies aim to address concerns regarding the public visibility of transactions while maintaining blockchain technology's security and integrity.

History and evolution of cryptocurrencies

Cryptocurrencies have come a long way since the inception of Bitcoin in 2009. In this section, we will explore the captivating history and evolution of cryptocurrencies, tracing their origins, significant milestones, and the transformative impact they have had on the financial landscape. From the birth of Bitcoin to the emergence of alternative cryptocurrencies and the development of blockchain technology, we will delve into the key events and trends that have shaped the evolution of cryptocurrencies into a global phenomenon.

Before delving into the history of cryptocurrencies, it is essential to acknowledge the early concepts and technologies that paved the way for their development.

The roots of cryptocurrencies can be traced back to the cypherpunk movement of the 1980s and 1990s. Cypherpunks were a group of activists and technologists who advocated for privacy-enhancing technologies and cryptography as a means to protect individual freedoms. They laid the ideological foundation for the development of decentralized digital currencies, emphasizing the need for secure and private financial transactions.

Several attempts were made to create digital currencies before Bitcoin. Examples include David Chaum's eCash and Wei Dai's b-money, both proposed in the 1990s. These early digital currencies aimed to provide privacy and security in online transactions, but they faced challenges in achieving widespread adoption and creating a decentralized system.

A turning point in the history of cryptocurrencies was the launch of Bitcoin in 2009. The creation of Bitcoin, under the pseudonym Satoshi Nakamoto, brought together various technologies and concepts to form a decentralized digital currency.

Satoshi Nakamoto released the Bitcoin whitepaper in October of 2008, with the title "Bitcoin: A Peer-to-Peer Electronic Cash System." This seminal document outlined the core principles and technical foundations of Bitcoin, including the use of blockchain technology, proof-of-work consensus mechanism, and the concept of a decentralized peer-to-peer network.

The genesis block, also known as Block 0, was mined on January 3, 2009, officially launching the Bitcoin network. This marked the creation of the first-ever bitcoin and the beginning of the Bitcoin blockchain. The mining process, involving computational power to solve complex mathematical problems, was introduced to secure the network and validate transactions.

Bitcoin gained attention within online communities, particularly among technologists, cypherpunks, and early adopters. The first notable transaction occurred in 2010 when Bitcoin was used to purchase two pizzas for 10,000 BTC. Over time, developers and enthusiasts contributed to the growth of the Bitcoin ecosystem, improving its functionalities and expanding its use cases.

Following the introduction of Bitcoin, alternative cryptocurrencies, commonly referred to as altcoins, started to emerge. Altcoins sought to address perceived limitations of Bitcoin and explore different features and use cases.

Namecoin, introduced in 2011, was one of the earliest altcoins. It aimed to create a decentralized domain name system (DNS) by combining blockchain technology with the registration of domain names. Namecoin pioneered the concept of using a blockchain for purposes beyond digital currency.

In 2011, Charlie Lee created Litecoin, often referred to as the "silver" to Bitcoin's "gold." Litecoin introduced a different hashing algorithm called Scrypt, which allowed for faster block generation and transaction confirmation times compared to Bitcoin. Litecoin served as an alternative digital currency with improved efficiency.

Ripple, launched in 2012, aimed to revolutionize the traditional banking system by enabling fast, low-cost international money transfers. Ripple introduced its own digital currency, XRP, and developed the Ripple protocol, a decentralized network for secure and efficient cross-border transactions.

Ethereum, introduced in 2015 by Vitalik Buterin, revolutionized the cryptocurrency landscape by introducing smart contracts. Smart contracts are self-executing contracts with predefined conditions written into code. Ethereum's blockchain platform allowed developers to create decentralized applications (DApps) and enabled the crowdfunding of projects through initial coin offerings (ICOs).

The proliferation of cryptocurrencies led to increased interest in the underlying technology that powers them: blockchain. The potential applications of blockchain technology extended beyond digital currency, with various sectors exploring its transformative capabilities.

The ability of blockchain technology to simplify procedures, improve security, and reduce costs has been acknowledged by the financial sector. Blockchain-based solutions emerged in areas such as supply chain management, identity verification, remittances, and decentralized finance (DeFi). The emergence of blockchain consortia and collaborations between industry players further fueled the development and adoption of blockchain technology.

Cryptocurrency exchanges have evolved as venues for buying, selling, and exchanging digital assets as cryptocurrencies have grown in popularity. Exchanges provided liquidity and a marketplace for individuals and institutions to engage in cryptocurrency transactions. The growth of exchanges facilitated the expansion of the cryptocurrency market, attracting investors, speculators, and businesses.

As cryptocurrencies became more prominent, regulatory frameworks started to evolve. Governments and financial authorities grappled with how to regulate this new asset class. While some jurisdictions embraced cryptocurrencies and blockchain technology, others imposed restrictions or implemented regulations to ensure consumer protection and combat illicit activities. Furthermore, institutional players, including banks, investment firms, and major corporations, began exploring cryptocurrency investments and integrating blockchain technology into their operations.

The history of cryptocurrencies has been marked by rapid evolution and continuous innovation. Looking ahead, several trends are shaping the future of cryptocurrencies and their potential impact on the global economy.

Decentralized Finance (DeFi) represents a growing movement within the cryptocurrency space, seeking to revolutionize traditional financial systems by providing decentralized alternatives to traditional financial intermediaries. DeFi encompasses various applications, such as lending, borrowing, decentralized exchanges, and yield farming, all powered by smart contracts and blockchain technology.

Central banks worldwide have recognized the potential of digital currencies and blockchain technology. Many countries are exploring the development of their own central bank digital currencies (CBDCs), which aim to combine the benefits of cryptocurrencies with the oversight and stability of centralized monetary systems. CBDCs have the potential to transform financial systems, improve financial inclusion, and enhance cross-border transactions.

As cryptocurrencies gain wider adoption, the need for scalable and interoperable solutions becomes paramount. Projects are actively exploring layer-two solutions, such as the Lightning Network for Bitcoin, to increase transaction throughput and reduce fees. Interoperability protocols, such as Polkadot and Cosmos, aim to connect different blockchains, enabling seamless communication and the transfer of assets across multiple networks.

Types of cryptocurrencies (Bitcoin, Ethereum, etc.)

Cryptocurrencies have witnessed a significant surge in popularity and diversification since the inception of Bitcoin in 2009. In this section, we will explore some of the most prominent types of cryptocurrencies, focusing on Bitcoin and Ethereum as representative examples. We will delve into their unique features, use cases, and underlying technologies, as well as introduce other notable cryptocurrencies that have made an impact in the digital currency landscape. By understanding the different types of cryptocurrencies, we can grasp the breadth and diversity of this rapidly evolving ecosystem.

Bitcoin, introduced by Satoshi Nakamoto in 2009, is widely regarded as the first and most well-known cryptocurrency. It laid the foundation for subsequent digital currencies and established the principles that underpin the entire cryptocurrency ecosystem.

Bitcoin operates on a decentralized network known as the Bitcoin blockchain. The blockchain technology that underpins Bitcoin functions as a distributed ledger that logs all transactions in a way that is both open and secure. This decentralized architecture ensures that no single entity or authority controls the Bitcoin network, enhancing security, transparency, and resilience to censorship.

For the purpose of validating transactions and ensuring the blockchain's continued integrity, Bitcoin makes use of a consensus method that is known as proof-of-work, or PoW. Miners compete to solve complex mathematical puzzles, and the first miner to find a solution is rewarded with newly minted Bitcoins. This PoW consensus mechanism provides security against fraudulent transactions and maintains the decentralized nature of the network.

There is a limited number of Bitcoins available, with a limitation of 21 million coins. This limited supply introduces scarcity and makes Bitcoin akin to digital gold. The controlled issuance of new Bitcoins through mining ensures that the currency remains deflationary, which, coupled with growing adoption, has led to the potential for value appreciation over time.

Ethereum, introduced by Vitalik Buterin in 2015, is a groundbreaking blockchain platform that goes beyond digital currency. Ethereum's distinguishing feature is its ability to execute smart contracts, enabling the creation of decentralized applications (DApps) and facilitating programmable and self-executing agreements.

Because they are written in code, smart contracts automatically carry out their terms and conditions. They automatically execute predefined conditions when certain criteria are met. Smart contracts can be executed on Ethereum's blockchain, allowing programmers to build a variety of decentralized apps and innovative solutions. This programmability has expanded the scope of blockchain technology beyond financial transactions, unlocking a vast array of potential use cases.

The cryptocurrency that runs exclusively on the Ethereum platform, ether (ETH), is used to power DApps and execute smart contracts. The Ethereum network requires processing resources and transaction fees, both of which are covered by Ethereum. These transaction fees, often referred to as gas fees, ensure that the network operates smoothly and discourages malicious activities. The Ethereum platform's security and stability are greatly enhanced by the gas fee mechanism.

Ethereum has been a driving force behind the rise of decentralized finance (DeFi), a movement seeking to revolutionize traditional financial systems through blockchain technology. DeFi encompasses various applications, including lending platforms, decentralized exchanges, and yield farming protocols. These DeFi solutions leverage Ethereum's smart contract functionality to provide transparent, permissionless, and efficient financial services to users worldwide.

Beyond Bitcoin and Ethereum, the cryptocurrency landscape is teeming with a diverse range of digital assets, each with its unique characteristics and use cases. Let us explore some notable alternative cryptocurrencies that have made a significant impact.

Ripple (XRP) aims to transform cross-border payments and facilitate fast and low-cost transactions. It provides a global payment protocol and cryptocurrency (XRP) that enables financial institutions to settle transactions quickly and securely. Ripple's focus on interoperability and efficiency has garnered attention from traditional financial institutions seeking to streamline their international payment processes.

Litecoin (LTC), often known as the "silver" to Bitcoin's "gold," has many similarity to Bitcoin but also introduces a number of significant differences. Litecoin offers faster transaction confirmation times and a different cryptographic algorithm called Scrypt, which favors high-speed memory rather than computational power. Litecoin's faster block generation time and increased transaction capacity make it suitable for day-to-day transactions.

A blockchain platform called Cardano (ADA) intends to offer a safe and expandable foundation for the creation of decentralized applications and smart contracts. It combines rigorous academic research with a layered architecture, ensuring scalability, security, and sustainability. Cardano's approach emphasizes peer-reviewed research and aims to strike a balance between regulatory compliance and privacy.

Polkadot (DOT) is a multi-chain platform that enables different blockchains to interoperate and share information seamlessly. It facilitates the transfer of assets and data across multiple chains, allowing for interoperability and collaboration between distinct blockchain networks. Polkadot's architecture promotes scalability, security, and innovation, opening up possibilities for cross-chain applications and collaborations.

The proliferation of cryptocurrencies and their underlying technologies has had a transformative impact on the financial landscape and beyond. As these digital assets continue to evolve and mature, their potential implications are far-reaching.

By giving the unbanked and underbanked populations around the world access to financial services, cryptocurrencies have the potential to promote financial inclusion. The ability to conduct peer-to-peer transactions without intermediaries empowers individuals who lack access to traditional banking services, enabling them to participate in the global economy.

Beyond the financial industry, blockchain technology and cryptocurrencies have the potential to disrupt numerous other industries. Supply chain management, healthcare, voting systems, and intellectual property are among the sectors investigating distributed ledgers' disruptive potential to improve efficiency, security, and transparency.

The need for interoperability and scalability solutions has become increasingly evident as cryptocurrencies gain wider adoption. Projects are actively working on interoperability protocols and layer-two solutions to address the challenges of scalability, ensuring that blockchain networks can handle higher transaction volumes and provide seamless communication between different chains.

Blockchain technology and its role in cryptocurrencies

Blockchain technology has emerged as a revolutionary innovation that underpins cryptocurrencies and has the potential to disrupt various industries. In this section, we will explore the intricacies of blockchain technology, its fundamental principles, and its vital role in the realm of cryptocurrencies. We will delve into the decentralized nature of blockchain, its mechanisms for consensus and verification, and its impact on security, transparency, and trust within the cryptocurrency ecosystem. By understanding blockchain technology, we can grasp the foundation upon which cryptocurrencies operate and appreciate its transformative potential in various sectors.

Blockchain technology can be characterized as a decentralized, distributed ledger system that securely and openly records and validates transactions. It operates on a network of computers, known as nodes, where each node maintains a copy of the entire blockchain. The core principles of blockchain technology include decentralization, immutability, transparency, and cryptographic security.

Decentralization is a foundational concept of blockchain technology. Traditional systems rely on a centralized authority to manage and verify transactions. In contrast, blockchain operates on a peer-to-peer network, where every participant has access to a synchronized and immutable copy of the blockchain. This decentralized architecture eliminates the need for intermediaries, reduces reliance on a central authority, and enhances security, transparency, and resilience.

Along with the introduction of Bitcoin in 2009, the idea of blockchain technology was also introduced. Bitcoin's blockchain was the first practical implementation of a decentralized ledger, serving as a public record of all Bitcoin transactions. The blockchain technology behind Bitcoin brought to life the vision of a trustless, decentralized digital currency.

Blockchain relies on consensus mechanisms to ensure that all participants agree on the validity of transactions and the state of the ledger. Consensus mechanisms, such as proof-of-work (PoW) and proof-of-stake (PoS), enable nodes to reach a consensus without relying on a central authority. These mechanisms provide security against fraudulent activities and maintain the integrity of the blockchain.

Blockchain ensures transactional security through its consensus mechanism and cryptographic techniques. Transactions are verified and added to the blockchain through a process called mining (in PoW-based blockchains). It takes a lot of computational power for miners to compete to solve challenging mathematical puzzles. A block is uploaded to the blockchain whenever a puzzle has been solved, making the transaction a part of an unchangeable, permanent record.

The immutability and transparency of blockchain make it a powerful tool for cryptocurrencies. Once a transaction is recorded on the blockchain, it becomes practically impossible to alter or delete. This immutability ensures the integrity of the transaction history and builds trust within the cryptocurrency ecosystem. Additionally, the transparent nature of the blockchain allows anyone to independently verify the legitimacy of transactions, enhancing transparency and reducing the need for trust in third parties.

Blockchain organizes transactions into blocks, each containing a list of verified transactions. Blocks are linked together using cryptographic hash functions, which generate a unique string of characters based on the data within the block. The hash of each block includes the hash of the previous block, creating an unbroken chain of blocks, hence the term "blockchain." The use of hash functions ensures the immutability of the blockchain and makes it extremely difficult to tamper with the recorded data.

Blockchain achieves consensus through a distributed consensus mechanism, allowing nodes to agree on the state of the blockchain. Consensus algorithms ensure that all nodes reach agreement on the validity of transactions and the order in which they are added to the blockchain. This distributed consensus prevents double-spending and ensures the consistency and security of the blockchain across all participating nodes.

Blockchain employs cryptographic techniques to secure transactions and protect the integrity of the blockchain. Digital signatures are made using public-key cryptography, which authenticate the identity of participants and ensure the authenticity of transactions. Encryption techniques are used to secure data transmitted over the network, safeguarding the privacy and security of participants. These cryptographic security measures form the backbone of blockchain technology, providing trust and confidence within the cryptocurrency ecosystem.

Blockchain technology has paved the way for the development of decentralized applications (DApps). DApps are built on blockchain platforms, like Ethereum, and leverage the transparency, security, and immutability of blockchain to enable new types of applications. These applications can range from decentralized finance (DeFi) platforms to supply chain management, identity verification, and voting systems. By removing the need for intermediaries and enhancing security, DApps offer new possibilities for innovation and disruption across various sectors.

DAPPS - DECENTRALIZED APPLICATIONS

Smart contracts operate as self-executing agreements in which the terms are directly put into the program code. They automate and enforce the performance of contractual obligations, eliminating the need for intermediaries and reducing the potential for human error or manipulation. Smart contracts are executed on blockchain platforms, and their transparency and immutability ensure trust and enforceability. Ethereum's blockchain has been a leading platform for the development and execution of smart contracts.

Scalability has been a key challenge for blockchain technology. As adoption increases, the need for solutions that can handle high transaction volumes becomes paramount. Projects are actively working on layer-two solutions, such as the Lightning Network for Bitcoin and Ethereum's proposed upgrades like Ethereum 2.0, to improve scalability while maintaining the security and decentralization of the blockchain.

With the proliferation of different blockchain networks, the need for interoperability has become essential. Interoperability protocols, such as Polkadot and Cosmos, aim to connect distinct blockchains, enabling seamless communication and the transfer of assets across multiple networks. These cross-chain solutions foster collaboration, expand possibilities, and enhance the overall efficiency of blockchain technology.

Beyond cryptocurrencies, blockchain technology has the ability to disrupt many different industries. Its attributes, such as decentralization, immutability, and transparency, can enhance security, streamline processes, reduce costs, and promote trust in sectors like supply chain management, healthcare, finance, and governance. By removing intermediaries and establishing trust in peer-to-peer interactions, blockchain technology can reshape traditional business models and drive innovation.

CHAPTER II

Getting Started with Cryptocurrency Investing

Setting up a digital wallet

For safely storing and using cryptocurrencies, digital wallets have emerged as a crucial tool. In this section, we will provide a comprehensive guide to setting up a digital wallet, covering the key concepts, types of wallets, security considerations, and step-by-step instructions. Whether you're new to cryptocurrencies or an experienced investor, understanding how to set up and use a digital wallet is crucial for safeguarding your assets and participating in the exciting world of decentralized finance.

A digital wallet, usually referred to as a cryptocurrency wallet, is a piece of either hardware or software that enables users to securely store, manage, and conduct cryptocurrency transactions. Unlike traditional wallets, digital wallets do not physically store cryptocurrencies; instead, they store the cryptographic keys needed to access and manage the digital assets on the blockchain. Digital wallets utilize a pair of cryptographic keys: a public key and a private key. The public key serves as an address for receiving funds, while the private key is used to access and authorize transactions.

There are several types of digital wallets available to cater to different needs and preferences. Software wallets, such as desktop wallets and mobile wallets, are installed on computers or smartphones, providing convenient access to cryptocurrencies. Web wallets, accessed through web browsers, offer user-friendly interfaces but require caution due to their online nature. Hardware wallets, physical devices, provide the highest level of security by storing private keys offline. Paper wallets, involving the printing of keys on physical media, offer an offline and secure storage option.

When setting up a digital wallet, security considerations are of utmost importance. Creating a backup of the wallet's private keys or recovery seed phrase is essential to restore access in case of loss or damage. Enabling two-factor authentication (2FA) adds an extra layer of security by requiring a secondary authentication code. Regularly updating the wallet software and applying security patches is crucial to protect against vulnerabilities. Physical security measures must be taken to safeguard hardware wallets from theft or damage.

Choosing the right wallet is the first step. Research and compare different wallet providers, considering factors such as security features, compatibility, and ease of use. Download and install the software wallet or create an account for a web wallet following the provider's instructions. Set a strong password and create a backup of the private keys or recovery seed phrase. For hardware wallets, purchase a reputable device, follow the manufacturer's instructions to set it up, and securely store the recovery seed phrase.

To receive cryptocurrency, provide the public address associated with the wallet to the sender. For sending cryptocurrency, open the wallet interface, enter the recipient's public address and the desired amount, review the transaction details, and confirm. Regularly monitor your wallet's interface to view holdings and transaction history. Keep the wallet software up to date and stay informed about the latest security practices in the cryptocurrency industry.

Choosing a reliable cryptocurrency exchange

As the popularity and adoption of cryptocurrencies continue to grow, choosing a reliable cryptocurrency exchange is essential for individuals looking to buy, sell, and trade digital assets. With a multitude of exchanges available, it is crucial to select a platform that prioritizes security, offers a wide range of cryptocurrencies, provides a user-friendly interface, and ensures regulatory compliance. In this section, we will explore the factors to consider when selecting a reliable cryptocurrency exchange, the key features to look for, and the steps to take to make an informed decision.

Security should be a top priority when choosing a cryptocurrency exchange. The exchange should employ robust security measures, including encryption, two-factor authentication (2FA), cold storage for funds, and regular security audits. A reliable exchange should have a proven track record of safeguarding user funds and protecting against hacking attempts.

For investors and traders, having access to a large variety of cryptocurrencies is essential. A reliable exchange should support major cryptocurrencies like Bitcoin (BTC), Ethereum (ETH), and Ripple (XRP), as well as emerging altcoins. The more diverse the cryptocurrency offerings, the greater the flexibility and trading opportunities for users.

A user-friendly interface makes navigating the exchange platform intuitive and efficient. Features such as an easy-to-use trading interface, real-time market data, order placement options, and account management tools contribute to a positive user experience. A reliable exchange should prioritize simplicity and accessibility for users of all experience levels.

Compliance with regulatory requirements demonstrates the exchange's commitment to operating within legal frameworks. A reliable exchange should implement know-your-customer (KYC) and anti-money laundering (AML) procedures to ensure the legitimacy of user identities and transactions. Compliance with relevant financial regulations and licensing demonstrates a commitment to transparency and accountability.

Research the reputation and track record of the exchange before making a decision. Look for user reviews, news articles, and community discussions to gauge the exchange's reliability, customer satisfaction, and history of security incidents. A well-established and reputable exchange inspires trust and confidence among users.

Evaluate the security measures implemented by the exchange. Look for features such as two-factor authentication (2FA), encryption, multi-signature wallets, and cold storage for funds. Consider whether the exchange has a history of security breaches and how it responded to such incidents.

Liquidity and trading volume play a significant role in the trading experience. Higher liquidity ensures better price stability and faster execution of trades. Look for exchanges with high trading volumes, as they tend to offer more competitive prices and a vibrant trading community.

Examine the fee structure of the exchange, including deposit, withdrawal, and trading fees. Some exchanges charge a percentage fee on each transaction, while others may offer discounted fees based on trading volume or membership tiers. Consider how the fees align with your trading strategy and frequency.

Prompt and effective customer support is crucial when dealing with technical issues or account-related inquiries. Look for exchanges that offer multiple channels of support, such as email, live chat, or phone, and ensure they have a reputation for responsiveness and helpfulness.

Start by researching and comparing different cryptocurrency exchanges. Make a list of exchanges that align with your requirements, such as security features, available cryptocurrencies, user interface, fees, and customer support. Consider factors such as reputation, track record, and regulatory compliance.

Examine the security measures implemented by each exchange on your list. Look for features like two-factor authentication, encryption, cold storage for funds, and the exchange's history of security incidents. Prioritize exchanges with a strong emphasis on security and a proven track record of protecting user funds.

Consider the range of cryptocurrencies available on each exchange. Look for exchanges that offer a diverse selection of cryptocurrencies, including major coins and promising altcoins. The availability of a wide variety of cryptocurrencies enables you to access different investment opportunities.

Compare the fee structures of the exchanges, including deposit, withdrawal, and trading fees. Evaluate the fee percentages and how they align with your trading strategy and frequency. Take note of any discounts or benefits offered based on trading volume or membership tiers.

Evaluate the user experience offered by each exchange. Test the trading interface, explore available features, and consider the ease of navigation. Additionally, research the quality and responsiveness of customer support by reading user reviews and feedback.

Ensure that the exchanges you are considering comply with relevant financial regulations and licensing requirements. Look for exchanges that implement know-your-customer (KYC) and anti-money laundering (AML) procedures to ensure compliance and foster a secure trading environment.

Based on your research and evaluation, narrow down your list of exchanges to the most reliable options. Consider factors such as reputation, security, cryptocurrency offerings, fees, user experience, and regulatory compliance. Select the exchange that best aligns with your needs and priorities.

Once you have chosen a cryptocurrency exchange, regularly review its security practices and stay informed about any updates or changes. Keep track of security recommendations and implement additional security measures on your end, such as using strong and unique passwords, enabling 2FA, and being cautious of phishing attempts.

Keep up with the most recent news and developments in the cryptocurrency sector. Follow reliable sources, join community forums, and participate in discussions to stay updated on security practices, regulatory changes, and emerging trends. You can use this information to make wise judgments and adjust to the changing environment.

Importance of security and protecting your investments

In the digital age, where cryptocurrencies have gained significant traction, understanding the importance of security and protecting your investments has become paramount. Cryptocurrencies offer exciting opportunities, but they also come with inherent risks. This section explores the crucial role of security in the cryptocurrency space and provides insights into safeguarding your investments. We will look into the risks posed by cryptocurrencies, discuss practical security solutions, and emphasize the importance of safeguarding your digital assets.

Cryptocurrencies have become prime targets for hackers due to their decentralized and pseudonymous nature. Cybercriminals use a variety of strategies, including phishing assaults, malware, and social engineering, to get into victims' digital wallets and take their assets. It is difficult to retrieve the stolen funds due to the absence of centralized oversight and the irreversible nature of transactions.

Cryptocurrency exchanges act as intermediaries for trading and storing digital assets. However, these exchanges are susceptible to security breaches, as seen in numerous high-profile incidents in the past. Exchanges may suffer from hacking attempts, insider attacks, or inadequate security practices, leading to the loss of user funds.

The regulatory landscape surrounding cryptocurrencies is still evolving in many jurisdictions. Uncertainty regarding government regulations, legal frameworks, and taxation policies pose risks to cryptocurrency investors. Changes in regulations or legal actions against specific cryptocurrencies can impact their value and legality, potentially resulting in financial losses.

It's essential to create secure, unique passwords for your cryptocurrency accounts. Implementing Two-Factor Authentication (2FA) provides an additional layer of security by mandating that in order to access your accounts, you must also provide a second authentication factor, such as a code that is sent to your mobile device. This protects against unauthorized access even if your password is compromised.

Using hardware wallets or software wallets with robust security features is essential for safeguarding your digital assets. Hardware wallets, such as Ledger and Trezor, provide offline storage and enhanced protection against hacking attempts. Software wallets should be chosen carefully, ensuring they are reputable and regularly updated to address any security vulnerabilities.

Cold storage involves storing cryptocurrencies offline, disconnected from the internet. Methods like hardware wallets, paper wallets, or dedicated offline devices ensure protection against online threats. Cold storage is particularly effective for long-term asset storage, reducing the risk of hacking and unauthorized access.

Keeping your wallet software and other related applications up to date is crucial. Security patches that address identified vulnerabilities are frequently included in software updates. Staying current with the latest software versions helps mitigate the risk of exploitation by malicious actors.

Staying informed about potential risks, best practices, and emerging security threats is vital. Educate yourself on cryptocurrency security through reputable sources, community forums, and expert advice. By understanding the risks and staying vigilant, you can better protect your investments.

Cryptocurrencies represent significant investments, and protecting them is crucial for maintaining financial well-being. The loss of digital assets due to security breaches or negligence can have severe financial implications. Safeguarding your investments ensures the preservation of your hard-earned funds and potential future gains.

Cryptocurrencies offer users greater privacy compared to traditional financial systems. Protecting your investments helps maintain your personal privacy by minimizing the risk of unauthorized access, identity theft, and potential exposure of financial transactions.

Protecting your investments builds trust and confidence in the cryptocurrency ecosystem. When individuals take security seriously, it contributes to the overall stability and credibility of the market. Increased security measures promote a safer environment for all participants, attracting more users and fostering long-term growth.

Conduct a thorough risk analysis and due diligence before investing in cryptocurrency or utilizing particular platforms. Research the security practices of exchanges and wallets, read user reviews, and stay informed about potential risks. Take into consideration all relevant information before settling on a decision, and based your choice on respectable and trustworthy sources.

Diversify your cryptocurrency investments to reduce exposure to a single asset or exchange. Spreading investments across different cryptocurrencies and platforms mitigates the risk of substantial losses. Additionally, consider setting limits on investment amounts and establish stop-loss mechanisms to manage potential risks.

Continuously monitor your investments and accounts to detect any suspicious activity. Regularly review transactions, account balances, and login history. Implementing auditing procedures and actively tracking your investments can help identify security weaknesses or potential vulnerabilities.

Create backups of your wallet's private keys or recovery seed phrases. Store these backups securely in offline or encrypted storage locations. Having a recovery plan in place ensures that you can regain access to your investments in case of device loss, damage, or theft.

Conducting thorough research before investing

Cryptocurrency investing may be a thrilling and financially rewarding endeavor. However, it is essential to approach cryptocurrency investments with caution and conduct thorough research before committing funds. Because of the volatility and complexity of the cryptocurrency market, investors must be well-informed in order to make wise decisions. In this section, we will explore the importance of conducting thorough research before investing in cryptocurrencies, examine key aspects to consider during the research process, and highlight the benefits of an informed approach to cryptocurrency investments.

Cryptocurrency markets are known for their high volatility, rapid price fluctuations, and intricate dynamics. Thorough research helps investors understand market trends, identify potential risks, and make informed decisions to mitigate the inherent volatility and complexity of the cryptocurrency space.

Conducting research provides investors with insights into the risks associated with specific cryptocurrencies, exchanges, and investment strategies. It allows for a comprehensive assessment of the potential risks involved and helps develop risk management strategies to protect investments.

Research helps investors identify potential investment opportunities in the vast landscape of cryptocurrencies. Understanding the underlying technology, project fundamentals, market adoption, and future prospects enables investors to identify cryptocurrencies with strong growth potential.

Thoroughly examining the fundamentals of a cryptocurrency project is crucial. Evaluate the technology, its purpose, potential use cases, and the problem it aims to solve. Investigate the development team's expertise, community engagement, partnerships, and regulatory compliance. Assessing these factors provides insights into the long-term viability and potential success of the project.

Conducting market analysis helps investors understand the broader market dynamics and trends. Analyze market capitalization, trading volume, liquidity, and historical price movements of the cryptocurrency in question. Compare the performance of the cryptocurrency against competitors or similar projects to gain a better understanding of its market position.

Carefully read the cryptocurrency's whitepaper and related documentation. Whitepapers outline the project's technology, goals, and implementation strategies. Scrutinize the technical aspects, consensus mechanism, scalability, security measures, and any potential limitations or risks highlighted in the document.

Evaluate the credibility and expertise of the project's development team. Research their backgrounds, qualifications, and track records. Engage with the community surrounding the cryptocurrency project, participate in forums, and monitor discussions to gauge community sentiment and assess the level of support and enthusiasm for the project.

Consider the regulatory landscape and legal aspects of investing in the specific cryptocurrency. Research the regulatory environment in the project's jurisdiction and any potential legal challenges or risks. Stay updated on regulatory developments and compliance requirements to ensure investments align with legal frameworks.

Thorough research enables investors to identify and assess potential risks associated with specific cryptocurrencies. By understanding the risks, investors can implement risk mitigation strategies, such as diversification, setting stop-loss orders, and implementing proper portfolio management techniques.

Research empowers investors to make informed decisions based on a solid understanding of the cryptocurrency project, its market dynamics, and the overall investment landscape. Informed decision-making increases the likelihood of making prudent investment choices and minimizing impulsive or emotionally driven decisions.

By conducting thorough research, investors can identify cryptocurrencies with strong growth potential and promising investment opportunities. This enables them to capitalize on emerging trends, technological advancements, and market shifts, potentially maximizing their investment returns over time.

Research acts as a defense mechanism against scams and fraudulent schemes prevalent in the cryptocurrency space. Thoroughly researching a project, its team, and its credibility helps identify red flags and avoid fraudulent investments that could result in significant financial losses.

Rely on reputable sources of information when conducting research. Seek information from trustworthy cryptocurrency news outlets, official project channels, reputable financial websites, and academic papers. Avoid relying solely on social media or unverified sources for investment-related information.

Consulting experts or industry professionals can provide valuable insights and perspectives. Engage with professionals who possess in-depth knowledge of the cryptocurrency market, blockchain technology, and investment strategies. Their expertise can help validate research findings and provide guidance on investment decisions.

The cryptocurrency market is dynamic and constantly evolving. Continuously update your knowledge by staying informed about emerging trends, technological advancements, and regulatory developments. Adapt research strategies and investment approaches based on the evolving landscape to make well-informed decisions.

CHAPTER III

Fundamental Analysis
for Cryptocurrency Investing

Evaluating the team and project behind a cryptocurrency

Evaluating the team and project behind a cryptocurrency is a fundamental step in cryptocurrencies before making investment decisions. The team's expertise, project vision, and execution capabilities significantly impact a cryptocurrency's success and long-term viability. In this section, we will delve into the importance of evaluating the team and project, explore key criteria to consider during the evaluation process and highlight how a thorough assessment can guide investors towards more informed and successful investments.

The team behind a cryptocurrency plays a vital role in shaping the project's direction, development, and adoption. A strong and capable team can navigate challenges, drive innovation, and adapt to market dynamics, ensuring the project's long-term viability.

Investors place trust in the team's ability to deliver on promises and execute the project's vision. A reputable and credible team enhances investors' confidence, attracts partnerships, and fosters positive sentiment in the cryptocurrency community.

Evaluating the team and project helps investors identify potential risks and assess the likelihood of successful execution. A thorough assessment aids in identifying red flags, mitigating risks associated with inexperienced or unreliable teams, and avoiding fraudulent or scam projects.

Assess the team's composition, including the core development team, advisors, and key stakeholders. Evaluate their backgrounds, experience, and expertise in relevant domains such as blockchain technology, finance, software development, and industry-specific knowledge. A diverse team with a blend of technical and business skills inspires confidence in the project's capabilities.

Investigate the team's track record and past achievements. Research their involvement in previous projects, contributions to the cryptocurrency community, or industry recognition. Past successes indicate the team's ability to deliver and execute their vision.

Evaluate the team's transparency and communication practices. Look for clear and concise project documentation, regular updates, and engagement with the community through official communication channels. Transparent teams are accountable and foster trust among investors and stakeholders.

Assess the project's roadmap and vision. A well-defined roadmap demonstrates the team's strategic planning and execution capabilities. Evaluate the project's objectives, milestones, and timelines. A clear vision that aligns with market demands and showcases innovation is indicative of a strong project foundation.

Examine the project's partnerships and industry connections. Collaborations with reputable companies, strategic alliances, or advisory support from industry experts validate the project's potential and provide access to valuable resources and networks.

Analyze the team's engagement with the cryptocurrency community. Monitor their participation in forums, social media platforms, and community events. A responsive and engaged team demonstrates their commitment to the project and indicates a supportive ecosystem.

Thorough evaluation helps mitigate risks associated with unreliable or inexperienced teams. Identifying red flags, such as team members lacking relevant experience or credibility, can safeguard investments from potential failures or mismanagement.

A comprehensive evaluation empowers investors to make informed decisions. By understanding the team's capabilities, past achievements, and project vision, investors can assess the potential value and risks associated with the cryptocurrency. Informed decisions increase the likelihood of successful investments.

Evaluation builds confidence in the team's ability to execute the project's objectives. Because they are more certain that the project's goals will be achieved, investors are more likely to trust a team that has a track record of success.

A well-evaluated team and project attract community support and foster adoption. Positive sentiment surrounding a project leads to increased engagement, participation, and market demand. Community support is essential for long-term growth and project success.

Conduct thorough research using reliable sources of information, such as official project websites, whitepapers, and credible news outlets. Investigate the team's backgrounds, accomplishments, and their level of involvement in the cryptocurrency community.

Participate in cryptocurrency forums, social media groups, and community discussions related to the project. Community engagement provides valuable insights, perspectives, and firsthand experiences with the team and project.

Consult industry experts, advisors, or professionals with knowledge in the cryptocurrency field. Their expertise and insights can provide valuable guidance, validate research findings, and offer a broader perspective on the team's capabilities and project viability.

Attend cryptocurrency events and conferences where the team or project representatives may be present. Engaging with the team in person allows for direct interaction, questioning, and observation of their commitment and knowledge.

Continuously monitor the team's progress and performance. Stay updated on the project's milestones, partnerships, and community engagement. Regular updates indicate a committed team actively working towards achieving project goals.

Be prepared to adapt evaluation criteria and perspectives as the cryptocurrency landscape evolves. Stay informed about market trends, technological advancements, and regulatory changes that may impact the team and project's future prospects.

Understanding whitepapers and technical documentation

Cryptocurrencies have revolutionized the financial landscape, offering new possibilities for decentralized systems and digital transactions. To fully grasp the potential of these digital assets, it is crucial to understand the underlying technology and the vision behind each cryptocurrency project. Whitepapers and technical documentation serve as invaluable resources, providing comprehensive insights into cryptocurrencies' purpose, functionality, and potential. In this section, we explore the significance of understanding whitepapers and technical documentation, examine their structure and components, decipher complex concepts, and highlight the importance of evaluating the team and expertise behind the projects. By gaining proficiency in analyzing these documents, investors can confidently navigate the intricate world of cryptocurrencies and unlock the potential for financial success.

Whitepapers are foundational documents that outline a cryptocurrency project's purpose, goals, and technical details. They play a crucial role in understanding the value proposition and evaluating a project's potential. By examining whitepapers, investors can gain insight into a cryptocurrency's vision, feasibility, and market potential.

Whitepapers follow a standardized structure, providing essential information about the project. They typically consist of an executive summary, introduction, technology and architecture, use cases and applications, token economy and distribution, and a roadmap for future plans. Understanding each component helps investors grasp the project's purpose, technical underpinnings, and long-term vision.

Cryptocurrency whitepapers often contain complex technical concepts and terminology. To comprehend these concepts fully, investors must delve into the underlying principles of blockchain technology, consensus mechanisms, cryptographic algorithms, and smart contracts. Investors can evaluate the project's technical robustness and innovative potential by researching and understanding core concepts.

A cryptocurrency project's success is greatly influenced by the team working on it. Whitepapers often provide information about the core team members, their backgrounds, and their expertise. Evaluating the team's experience and track record enables investors to assess the project's potential for success and the team's ability to execute the proposed vision. Reviewing technical documentation, such as GitHub repositories and developer guides, provides insights into ongoing development progress and community engagement.

Investors should consider peer review and audits, which provide external validation of a project's security, code quality, and adherence to best practices. Comparing the whitepapers of competing projects within the same industry offers a broader perspective, allowing investors to assess a project's competitive advantage and potential for market adoption. Understanding a cryptocurrency project's regulatory landscape is crucial to ensure compliance and mitigate potential risks.

Understanding whitepapers and technical documentation is essential for making informed investment decisions in cryptocurrency. These documents provide valuable insights into cryptocurrencies' purpose, functionality, and potential. By delving into their structure, deciphering complex concepts, and evaluating the team and expertise, investors can confidently navigate the cryptocurrency landscape.

Whitepapers should be viewed as a starting point for due diligence; additional research is necessary. Engaging with the development community, consulting industry experts, and staying informed about regulatory changes further enhances understanding. By mastering the art of understanding whitepapers and technical documentation, investors can identify innovative projects, assess their potential, and participate in the digital revolution that cryptocurrencies bring.

Embrace the knowledge within these documents and unlock the potential for financial success in the ever-evolving world of cryptocurrencies. By harnessing the power of whitepapers and technical documentation, investors can navigate the intricacies of the cryptocurrency market and seize the opportunities that arise in this dynamic and transformative landscape.

Assessing market demand and adoption potential

Assessing market demand and adoption potential is a crucial step in understanding cryptocurrencies' viability and growth prospects. The cryptocurrency market is dynamic and driven by factors such as user adoption, technological advancements, regulatory developments, and market trends. This section will explore the significance of assessing market demand and adoption potential, discuss critical indicators to consider, and highlight the benefits of making informed assessments when venturing into cryptocurrency investments.

Assessing market demand and adoption potential enables investors to identify cryptocurrencies with significant growth prospects. Understanding the factors that drive demand and adoption allows for strategic investment decisions, maximizing the potential for long-term value appreciation.

Investing in cryptocurrencies carries inherent risks, including volatility and uncertainty. Assessing market demand and adoption potential helps investors identify projects that have gained traction and are more likely to withstand market fluctuations. It aids in mitigating risks associated with investing in projects with limited adoption or unclear market prospects.

Market demand and adoption potential provide insights into the long-term viability of cryptocurrencies. A project with solid market demand and widespread adoption has a higher likelihood of survival, sustainability, and potential future growth. Assessing these factors helps investors identify projects that are likely to thrive in the evolving cryptocurrency ecosystem.

Evaluate the size and engagement of the user base and community surrounding the cryptocurrency project. Look for indicators such as active forum participation, social media engagement, and a dedicated community. A large and engaged user base suggests growing interest and potential for widespread adoption.

Analyze the market capitalization and trading volume of the cryptocurrency. Higher market capitalization and trading volume indicate increased market demand and liquidity, making cryptocurrency more attractive to investors and traders. This can contribute to price stability and a vibrant trading environment.

Examine the project's partnerships and integrations with established companies or platforms. Collaborations with reputable organizations increase the credibility and adoption potential of the cryptocurrency. Partnerships can provide access to larger user bases, new markets, and enhanced functionality, driving adoption and demand.

Assess the technological advancements and innovations associated with cryptocurrency. Projects that introduce novel solutions, improve scalability, enhance security, or offer unique features have a higher potential for market demand and adoption. Technological advancements contribute to the project's competitive advantage and value proposition.

Evaluate the cryptocurrency's regulatory compliance and adherence to legal frameworks. Projects that demonstrate compliance with relevant regulations inspire trust and confidence among users and institutional investors. Clear compliance measures facilitate widespread adoption by removing regulatory barriers.

Consider the presence and growth of real-world use cases for cryptocurrency. Evaluate whether the project solves practical problems, addresses industry pain points, or enables innovative applications. Real-world use cases validate the utility and demand for cryptocurrency in various sectors, indicating its adoption potential.

Assessing market demand and adoption potential allows investors to make informed investment decisions. By understanding the factors driving demand and adoption, investors can identify cryptocurrencies with growth potential, allocate resources strategically, and optimize investment returns.

Thorough assessments of market demand and adoption potential help mitigate investment risks. By focusing on projects with established market demand and adoption, investors reduce the likelihood of investing in projects with limited viability or high volatility. This risk mitigation strategy contributes to a more resilient investment portfolio.

Informed assessments uncover investment opportunities that align with market trends and emerging technologies. Identifying projects with strong market demand and adoption potential enables investors to position themselves at the forefront of technological advancements, increasing the likelihood of capitalizing on future market growth.

Assessing market demand and adoption potential allows investors to identify promising early-stage projects. Investing in these projects at an early stage offers the potential for significant returns as the project gains momentum and broader adoption. Early identification maximizes investment opportunity.

Conduct comprehensive research and market analysis to understand the landscape and trends of the cryptocurrency market. Stay informed about industry news, technological advancements, regulatory changes, and emerging use cases. Evaluate market dynamics to identify potential growth areas and investment opportunities.

Monitor user feedback and sentiment surrounding the cryptocurrency project. Use discussion boards, social media, and forums to interact with the community and learn more about their passion, issues, and adoption experiences. User feedback provides valuable insights into market demand and user experience.

Monitor key adoption metrics, such as the number of active wallets, transaction volume, merchant adoption, and cryptocurrency integration into existing platforms or ecosystems. Tracking these metrics helps assess the growth and adoption potential of the cryptocurrency project.

Analyze market trends, competitor projects, and industry developments. Assess how the cryptocurrency project stands out in terms of technology, use cases, partnerships, and market positioning.

Understanding the competitive landscape provides insights into the project's potential to capture market demand and gain traction.

Market demand and adoption potential are subject to change as the cryptocurrency ecosystem evolves. Monitor market trends, user feedback, regulatory changes, and technological advancements. Regularly reassess the project's market demand and adoption potential to adapt investment strategies accordingly.

Remain flexible and open to adjusting investment decisions based on emerging trends and new information. Embrace a learning mindset, continuously expanding knowledge, and seeking expert opinions to stay informed and make well-informed assessments.

Analyzing partnerships and collaborations

Collaborations and partnerships are essential to the development and success of cryptocurrency projects. Cryptocurrencies gain access to new markets, resources, and expertise by forming strategic alliances, propelling their adoption and market value. This section will explore the significance of analyzing partnerships and collaborations, discuss their benefits to cryptocurrency projects, and outline key factors to consider when evaluating these alliances.

Partnerships and collaborations allow cryptocurrency projects to expand their presence in new markets. By leveraging established partnerships, projects can access a broader user base, driving user adoption and increasing demand for cryptocurrency.

Collaborations bring access to valuable resources and expertise. Partnerships with established companies, institutions, or industry experts provide cryptocurrency projects with funding, technological support, marketing know-how, and regulatory guidance. These resources accelerate project development and enhance its market competitiveness.

Forming partnerships with reputable entities or industry leaders bolsters the credibility and trustworthiness of cryptocurrency projects. Collaborating with well-known organizations helps build confidence among users, investors, and the wider community, thereby attracting more adoption and investment.

Partnerships and collaborations enhance the visibility of cryptocurrency projects in the market. Joint marketing efforts, co-branding initiatives, and shared resources enable projects to reach a larger audience, improving brand recognition and attracting new users.

Collaborations facilitate the exchange of knowledge and technology between cryptocurrency projects and their partners. This enables projects to integrate new technologies, leverage innovative solutions, and stay at the forefront of industry developments. Access to cutting-edge technologies enhances the project's value proposition and competitiveness.

Partnerships with established exchanges or liquidity providers enhance trading opportunities for the cryptocurrency. By securing listings on reputable exchanges, projects gain exposure to a broader range of traders and investors, boosting liquidity and potentially increasing the value of the cryptocurrency.

Collaborating with regulatory experts or legal advisors helps cryptocurrency projects navigate complex regulatory environments. Partnerships provide insights into compliance requirements, ensure adherence to regulatory standards, and mitigate legal risks, fostering a favorable environment for adoption and growth.

Evaluate whether the partnership aligns with the project's objectives and long-term vision. The goals and values of both parties should be complementary, ensuring a mutually beneficial collaboration that supports the growth and success of the cryptocurrency project.

Assess the reputation and track record of potential partners. Consider their history of successful collaborations, the quality of their previous projects, and their standing within the industry. A partner with a solid reputation enhances the credibility and trustworthiness of the cryptocurrency project.

Examine the expertise that the partner brings to the collaboration. Consider their experience, technical knowledge, and industry connections. A partner with complementary skills can provide valuable guidance, resources, and access to networks that strengthen the cryptocurrency project.

Evaluate the partner's market reach and user base. Assess whether the collaboration opens doors to new user segments, expands the project's market presence, or taps into previously untapped markets.

A partner with a substantial user base enhances the project's potential for widespread adoption.

Consider the long-term viability of the partnership. Assess the partner's stability and commitment, financial health, and willingness to invest resources in the collaboration. A partner with a long-term perspective and commitment to the project ensures sustainability and continuity of support.

Evaluate the impact of partnerships on user adoption and engagement. Monitor metrics such as user growth, user activity, and user feedback. Assess whether the collaboration has increased users, improved user experience, or expanded user functionalities.

Analyze the market expansion resulting from partnerships. Measure the project's penetration into new markets, the growth of its user base in those markets, and its brand recognition. Determine whether the partnership has successfully positioned the project for broader adoption.

Quantify the financial benefits of partnerships. Assess whether the collaboration has resulted in increased trading volume, enhanced liquidity, or a positive impact on the value of the cryptocurrency. Analyze market data and trading patterns to determine the partnership's financial success.

Monitor the integration of technologies resulting from partnerships. Assess whether the collaboration has successfully integrated new technologies, improved scalability, or enhanced functionality.

Evaluate how the partnership has contributed to the project's technological advancements.

Conduct thorough due diligence on potential partners. Research their reputation, previous collaborations, market positioning, and financial stability. Engage in discussions and negotiations to ensure alignment of goals and objectives.

Engage in industry networking events, conferences, and online forums to identify potential partners. Building relationships and staying connected with industry leaders and experts enhances the chances of identifying mutually beneficial collaboration opportunities.

Continuously evaluate partnerships and collaborations to ensure they align with the evolving needs and goals of the cryptocurrency project. Be open to adapting strategies and seeking new partnerships as the project and market dynamics change.

CHAPTER IV

Technical Analysis for Cryptocurrency Investing

Introduction to technical analysis tools and indicators

Technical analysis tools and indicators are essential for investors and traders navigating the dynamic and often volatile cryptocurrency market. These tools enable the analysis of historical price data, market trends, and patterns to make informed investment decisions.

This section will explore the significance of technical analysis, discuss essential tools and indicators, and highlight how they can empower investors to identify opportunities and enhance trading strategies in the cryptocurrency market.

Technical analysis provides insights into market trends by examining historical price and volume data. It helps investors identify patterns, trends, and market cycles, allowing them to anticipate potential price movements and make informed trading decisions.

Technical analysis assists investors in determining optimal entry and exit points for their trades. By identifying key support and resistance levels, investors can enter positions when the price is expected to rise and exit before a potential reversal occurs, maximizing profit potential.

The technical analysis aids in risk management by setting stop-loss orders and profit targets based on support and resistance levels. By defining these levels, investors can mitigate losses and secure profits, enhancing overall portfolio performance.

Candlestick charts display price data in a graphical form, visually representing price movements over a specific period. Candlestick patterns such as doji, hammer, and engulfing patterns offer insights into market sentiment and potential trend reversals.

Moving averages smooth out price data over a specified period, highlighting trends and providing support and resistance levels. The most common types of moving averages are the simple moving average (SMA) and the exponential moving average (EMA). Moving averages help identify price trends and potential entry or exit points.

A momentum oscillator called the Relative Strength Index (RSI) gauges the rapidity and variety of price changes. Its readings, which range from 0 to 100, are overbought at values above 70 and oversold at values below 30. The RSI helps investors identify potential trend reversals and assess the strength of price movements.

A simple moving average (SMA) and two standard deviation lines that are positioned above and below the SMA make up Bollinger Bands. Bollinger Bands provide insights into price volatility and potential trend reversals. The price may indicate overbought conditions when it touches the upper band, while touching the lower band may indicate oversold conditions.

Based on Fibonacci ratios, Fibonacci retracement levels are horizontal lines that represent possible levels of support and resistance. These levels are drawn between the high and low points of a price movement, helping identify potential price reversal zones or areas of consolidation.

Volume analysis assesses the trading volume accompanying price movements. High volume during price increases or decreases confirms the trend's strength, while low volume may indicate weak market participation. Volume analysis provides insights into market sentiment and helps ensure trend reversals.

Technical analysis tools and indicators empower investors to make informed decisions based on historical price patterns and market trends. By utilizing these tools, investors can develop trading strategies backed by data, increasing the likelihood of successful trades and maximizing profits.

Technical analysis tools enable investors to identify optimal entry and exit points. By analyzing price patterns, support and resistance levels, and indicators, investors can time their trades to take advantage of potential price movements, improving trade execution and minimizing risks.

The technical analysis aids in risk management by setting appropriate stop-loss orders and profit targets. By identifying essential support and resistance levels, investors can determine the level at which to exit a trade to limit potential losses. This helps protect capital and minimize risks.

Utilizing technical analysis tools instills confidence and conviction in investors' decisions. By analyzing price patterns, trends, and indicators, investors gain a deeper understanding of market dynamics, enabling them to make decisions based on data rather than emotions or impulses.

Use a combination of technical indicators to validate signals and confirm market trends. Combining indicators such as moving averages, RSI, and Bollinger Bands can provide a more comprehensive view of the market, increasing the accuracy of the analysis.

Select the appropriate timeframe based on trading objectives. Short-term traders may focus on intraday or hourly charts, while long-term investors may analyze daily or weekly charts. Choosing a suitable timeframe aligns the analysis with the desired trading strategy.

Backtesting involves applying technical analysis tools and indicators to historical price data to evaluate their effectiveness. By testing different strategies and indicators on past data, investors can gain insights into their performance and refine their trading approach.

Implement proper risk and money management strategies to protect capital and optimize returns. Set appropriate stop-loss orders, calculate position sizes based on risk tolerance, and adhere to a disciplined approach to avoid excessive losses.

Recognize that technical analysis tools and indicators should adapt to changing market conditions. Specific indicators may become more or less reliable as the cryptocurrency market evolves. Regularly reassess the effectiveness of tools and adjust strategies accordingly.

The field of technical analysis is constantly evolving. Stay updated on new indicators, patterns, and strategies by reading reputable literature, following expert analysis, and participating in educational programs. Continuous learning enhances analytical skills and improves decision-making.

Reading and interpreting cryptocurrency charts

Cryptocurrency charts provide a window into the dynamic world of digital asset trading. Reading and interpreting these charts is a fundamental skill for investors and traders, enabling them to analyze price movements, identify trends, and make informed trading decisions. In this section, we will explore the significance of reading and interpreting cryptocurrency charts, discuss key elements of chart analysis, and highlight how mastering this skill can unlock opportunities in the cryptocurrency market.

Cryptocurrency charts reveal the ongoing price discovery process and enable the identification of trends. Traders can discern patterns, support and resistance levels, and market trends by studying historical price movements. This information helps in forecasting future price movements and making informed trading decisions.

Reading and interpreting cryptocurrency charts aids in determining optimal entry and exit points for trades. Chart analysis allows traders to identify potential price reversals, breakouts, and trend continuations. Timing entry and exit points correctly enhance profitability and risk management.

Cryptocurrency charts reflect market sentiment and investor psychology. By examining patterns and candlestick formations, traders can gauge the emotions of market participants—such as fear, greed, or indecision. Understanding market sentiment facilitates better decision-making and risk assessment.

Cryptocurrency charts are available in various timeframes, including minute-based (e.g., 1-minute, 5-minute), hourly, daily, weekly, and monthly. Different timeframes provide different levels of detail and are suited for various trading strategies. Short-term traders may focus on lower timeframes, while long-term investors may analyze higher timeframes.

Candlestick patterns represent the price action within a given timeframe. They provide insights into market sentiment and potential trend reversals. Common candlestick patterns include doji, hammer, shooting star, and engulfing patterns. These patterns help traders anticipate market movements and make decisions accordingly.

Price levels that have historically seen buying or selling pressure for cryptocurrencies are known as support and resistance levels. Support acts as a floor, preventing prices from falling further, while resistance acts as a ceiling, preventing prices from rising further. Identifying these levels assists traders in making decisions related to entry, exit, and stop-loss placement.

Moving averages smooth out price data over a specific period, providing a trend line that helps traders identify the market's overall direction. Two forms of moving averages that are widely used are simple moving averages (SMA) and exponential moving averages (EMA). Moving averages aid trend identification, crossovers, and potential support or resistance levels.

Volume analysis examines the trading volume accompanying price movements. High volume during price increases or decreases confirms the strength of the trend, while low volume may indicate weak market participation. Volume analysis helps traders validate price movements and assess market sentiment.

By examining the price action on the chart, you can identify the dominant trend. In an uptrend, look for higher highs and higher lows, while in a downtrend, look for lower highs and lower lows.

Identifying the trend direction assists in aligning trading strategies with the overall market sentiment.

Locate key support and resistance levels by identifying areas where price has historically reversed or consolidated. These levels act as potential entry or exit points and areas to place stop-loss orders. Observing how price reacts at these levels can provide insights into market dynamics.

Study candlestick patterns to understand market sentiment and potential trend reversals. Learn to recognize patterns such as doji, hammer, and engulfing patterns, as they often indicate a shift in market direction. Combining candlestick patterns with other technical indicators enhances the accuracy of chart analysis.

Combine multiple technical indicators to validate signals and confirm market trends. For example, if a moving average crossover aligns with a breakout from a resistance level, it strengthens the potential trade setup. Using multiple indicators enhances the robustness of analysis and reduces false signals.

Reading and interpreting cryptocurrency charts gives traders the information needed to make informed trading decisions. Analyzing price patterns, support and resistance levels, and other technical indicators empowers traders to enter trades with a higher probability of success and manage risks effectively.

By understanding chart patterns and support/resistance levels, traders can set appropriate stop-loss orders and manage risk effectively.

Based on chart analysis, setting stop-loss orders at logical levels reduces potential losses and protects capital.

Accurate chart analysis enables traders to time their entry and exit points effectively. Identifying potential price reversals, breakouts, or trend continuations assists in entering positions at favorable prices and maximizing profit potential.

Mastering chart analysis instills confidence in traders' decision-making. Traders get a sense of control and are less likely to be influenced by brief market changes or emotions by knowing price movements and market trends.

Continuously learn and expand your knowledge of different chart patterns. Familiarize yourself with common patterns and their implications. Regularly review historical charts to enhance pattern recognition skills.

Stay informed about market news, industry developments, and regulatory changes. Understanding external factors that influence price movements can enhance the accuracy of chart analysis.

Backtest trading strategies using historical data to evaluate their effectiveness. Maintain a trading journal to record trades, observations, and lessons learned. Reviewing past trades and analyzing their outcomes aids in refining trading strategies.

Engage in online forums, social media communities, and trading groups to learn from experienced traders. Seek mentorship or guidance from professionals with expertise in chart analysis and successful trading.

Identifying trends, support, and resistance levels

Identifying trends, support, and resistance levels is a fundamental skill for investors and traders in the cryptocurrency market. These elements provide valuable insights into market dynamics, enabling traders to make informed decisions regarding entry and exit points, risk management, and overall trading strategies. In this section, we will delve into the significance of identifying trends, support, and resistance levels, discuss the fundamental techniques and indicators used for analysis, and highlight the benefits of mastering this skill in the cryptocurrency trading realm.

Identifying trends is crucial for understanding the overall market direction. By analyzing price data over different timeframes, traders can ascertain whether the market is in an uptrend, downtrend, or consolidation phase. This knowledge helps traders align their strategies with the prevailing trend, enhancing the probability of successful trades.

Identifying support and resistance levels aids traders in making informed decisions regarding entry and exit points. Support levels act as a price floor, where buying pressure typically prevents prices from falling further. On the other hand, resistance levels act as a price ceiling, where selling pressure tends to prevent prices from rising. Timing trades based on these levels optimize risk-reward ratios and enhances trade execution.

Support and resistance levels also play a critical role in risk management. By setting appropriate stop-loss orders based on these levels, traders can mitigate potential losses and protect their capital. Stop-loss orders are placed just below support levels for buy trades and just above resistance levels for sell trades, reducing the impact of adverse price movements.

Trendlines are drawn by connecting consecutive higher lows in an uptrend or consecutive lower highs in a downtrend. They visually represent the trend and can help traders identify potential trend reversals or continuations. Trendlines act as dynamic support or resistance levels.

Moving averages smooth out price data over a specific period, revealing the average price within that timeframe. Traders commonly use the simple moving average (SMA) or the exponential moving average (EMA) to identify trends and potential support or resistance levels. Moving averages provide a clearer picture of price direction by filtering out short-term fluctuations.

Fibonacci retracement levels are based on mathematical ratios derived from the Fibonacci sequence. These levels help identify potential support and resistance levels by measuring the retracement of a price move. Traders draw Fibonacci retracement lines from swing lows to swing highs in an uptrend and vice versa in a downtrend.

The high, low, and closing prices from the previous day are used to establish pivot points, which are levels of support and resistance.

These levels help traders anticipate potential price movements by providing reference points for price reversals or continuations. Pivot points are beneficial in short-term trading and day trading strategies.

Volume analysis assesses the trading volume accompanying price movements. Higher volume during price increases or decreases indicates more robust market participation and confirms the validity of the trend. Volume analysis provides insights into the strength of support and resistance levels and helps traders validate price movements.

The visual analysis involves observing price patterns and trends on cryptocurrency charts. In an uptrend, traders look for higher highs and higher lows; in a downtrend, they look for lower highs and lower lows; and in sideways markets, they look for consolidation patterns. Visual analysis is the foundation of trend identification and support/resistance level determination.

Examining price charts across different timeframes provides a comprehensive view of the market. Shorter periods, such as hourly or 15-minute charts, highlight intraday price movements and potential support/resistance levels, while longer timeframes, such as daily or weekly charts, aid in the identification of key patterns. Multiple timeframe analysis confirms trends and levels across different scales.

Analyzing historical price data allows traders to identify recurring support and resistance levels. By studying previous price reactions at specific levels, traders can determine their significance and use them as reference points for future trades. Historical data analysis aids in identifying key levels that are likely to influence price movements.

Support and resistance levels can be verified by technical indicators like stochastic oscillators, RSI, or moving averages. For example, when price approaches a support level, and the RSI indicates oversold conditions, it provides additional validation for a potential price reversal. Using indicators in conjunction with visual analysis strengthens support and resistance level identification accuracy.

Accurately identifying trends, support, and resistance levels enables traders to time their trades effectively. By entering positions at or near support levels in an uptrend or resistance levels in a downtrend, traders increase the probability of profitable trades and maximize potential gains.

Identifying support and resistance levels aids in setting appropriate stop-loss orders. Placing stop-loss orders just below support levels for buy trades or above resistance levels for sell trades minimizes potential losses and protects capital. Effective risk management is crucial for long-term trading success.

Support and resistance levels serve as validation tools for trade setups. When a trade aligns with a significant support or resistance level, traders gain confidence in the trade's potential success. Validation increases conviction and discipline in executing trades.

Trend identification and support/resistance level analysis provide clarity in market analysis. By understanding the prevailing market direction and key levels, traders can filter out market noise and focus on relevant price action. A clear market analysis aids in making rational and objective trading decisions.

Continuously observe price charts and practice identifying trends, support, and resistance levels. Regular chart analysis improves pattern recognition skills and enhances the ability to identify reliable levels.

Maintain a trading journal to record observations, trades, and lessons learned. Regularly review past trades to analyze the accuracy of support and resistance level identification. Reflecting on previous trades facilitates continuous improvement.

Stay informed about market news, industry developments, and regulatory changes that may impact price movements. Understanding external factors helps traders interpret support and resistance levels in light of market dynamics.

Engage with experienced traders, participate in online forums, and attend educational programs to expand knowledge and seek guidance. Learning from professional traders enhances understanding and proficiency in identifying trends, support, and resistance levels.

Using moving averages, oscillators, and other indicators

In the dynamic world of cryptocurrency trading, understanding and effectively utilizing technical indicators is paramount to making informed trading decisions. Moving averages, oscillators, and other indicators provide valuable insights into market trends, momentum, and potential reversals. In this section, we will explore the significance of using these indicators in cryptocurrency trading, discuss key types of indicators, and highlight their benefits in enhancing trading strategies and profitability.

Technical indicators help traders identify market trends by analyzing price data. By understanding the prevailing trend, traders can align their strategies with the market direction, improving the accuracy of their trades and optimizing profit potential.

Indicators provide insights into market momentum, allowing traders to gauge the strength and speed of price movements. This information helps traders evaluate the conviction of market participants and identify potential entry or exit points.

Indicators assist in identifying potential trend reversals. By detecting divergences, overbought or oversold conditions, or pattern formations, traders can anticipate shifts in market sentiment and adjust their trading strategies accordingly.

Moving averages (MA) are widely used to identify trends, smooth out price data, and generate trading signals. The most common types of moving averages include the Simple Moving Average (SMA) and the Exponential Moving Average (EMA). Moving averages provide insights into the market's overall direction and potential support and resistance levels.

Oscillators are indicators that move within a defined range and show whether the market is overbought or oversold. Three popular oscillators include the moving average convergence divergence

(MACD), the stochastic oscillator, and the relative strength index (RSI). Oscillators help traders identify potential reversal points and assess market sentiment.

Volume indicators analyze trading volume alongside price movements to assess market participation. Examples of volume indicators include On-Balance Volume (OBV), Chaikin Money Flow (CMF), and Volume Weighted Average Price (VWAP). Volume indicators provide insights into the strength of price movements and potential trend reversals.

Trend-following indicators are designed to identify and confirm trends. Examples of trend-following indicators include the Average Directional Index (ADX), Parabolic SAR, and Ichimoku Cloud. These indicators assist traders in determining the strength of a trend and potential entry or exit points.

A technical method known as Fibonacci retracement uses Fibonacci ratios to identify probable support and resistance levels. Traders use this indicator to determine levels at which the price is likely to reverse or consolidate.

Technical indicators help traders time their trades more effectively. By identifying potential entry or exit points, traders can enter trades during favorable market conditions and improve their risk-to-reward ratio.

Indicators confirm price movements, reinforcing traders' analysis and validating trading signals. When multiple indicators align with the expected price direction, it increases traders' confidence in their trading decisions.

Technical indicators assist in risk management by setting appropriate stop-loss orders and profit targets. Traders can determine levels at which they should exit a trade to limit potential losses or secure profits, minimizing risk exposure.

Indicators serve as a foundation for developing trading strategies. By combining different indicators and analyzing their signals, traders can devise comprehensive strategies tailored to their trading style and risk tolerance.

Each technical indicator has its own characteristics and limitations. Traders must understand the interpretation and application of each indicator to avoid misinterpretation and false signals.

Combining multiple indicators can enhance the accuracy of analysis and trading signals. Traders often use a mix of trend-following indicators, oscillators, and volume indicators to gain a comprehensive view of the market and validate trading decisions.

Traders can customize indicator parameters to suit their trading style and market conditions. Adjusting parameters, such as the length of moving averages or the sensitivity of oscillators, can improve the relevance of signals and adapt to changing market dynamics.

Backtesting involves applying indicators to historical data to evaluate their effectiveness. Traders can assess the performance of indicators, test different strategies, and refine their trading approach based on the analysis of past data.

Traders should stay updated on market trends, industry news, and regulatory developments that may impact the effectiveness of indicators. Adapting to market changes ensures indicators remain relevant and effective.

Engaging with fellow traders, joining online forums, and seeking mentorship can accelerate learning and provide valuable insights into indicator usage and trading strategies. Learning from experienced traders fosters continuous growth and improvement.

Traders should regularly assess the performance of indicators by monitoring their accuracy and reliability. Removing or replacing ineffective indicators and incorporating new ones into the analysis can enhance trading strategies.

CHAPTER V

Building a Cryptocurrency Investment Strategy

Setting investment goals and risk tolerance

Successful cryptocurrency investing requires a well-defined investment strategy that aligns with individual goals and risk tolerance. Setting clear investment goals and understanding risk tolerance are crucial steps in navigating the volatile and fast-paced cryptocurrency market. In this section, we will explore the significance of setting investment goals and risk tolerance, discuss key considerations in goal setting, and highlight how aligning these factors can pave the way to successful cryptocurrency investing.

Setting investment goals provides clarity and direction to investors. Clear objectives help determine the desired outcomes of investment activities and serve as a benchmark for measuring progress and success. By defining investment goals, investors can focus on specific targets, such as capital appreciation, income generation, or portfolio diversification.

Setting investment goals helps manage expectations and reduces emotional decision-making. Investors with well-defined goals are less likely to be swayed by short-term market fluctuations or influenced by herd mentality. Establishing realistic expectations based on individual circumstances and risk appetite fosters disciplined and rational investment decisions.

Understanding risk tolerance allows investors to identify the level of risk they are comfortable with and willing to undertake. By aligning investment goals with risk tolerance, investors can create a portfolio that balances potential returns and risk exposure appropriately. This helps mitigate the potential negative impact of market volatility and unexpected events.

The time horizon is a critical factor in goal setting. Investors should consider whether their investment goals are short-term (less than a year), medium-term (1-5 years), or long-term (5 years or more). Time horizons influence the investment strategy, asset allocation, and risk tolerance required to achieve the goals within the specified timeframe.

Investment goals should align with an individual's financial needs and lifestyle. Whether it is saving for retirement, funding education expenses, or purchasing a home, understanding the financial requirements and determining the necessary investment returns is essential for goal setting. Investors should consider their income, expenses, and future obligations to ensure their goals are realistic and attainable.

Risk appetite refers to an individual's willingness to take on risk in pursuit of investment returns. Different investors have varying risk tolerances based on their financial situation, personal circumstances, and psychological makeup. Determining risk tolerance involves assessing one's capacity to withstand potential losses and volatility. Investors should objectively evaluate their comfort level with market fluctuations and adjust their investment strategy accordingly.

Setting investment goals provides a clear focus and direction for investors. Goals act as a guidepost, allowing investors to remain disciplined and committed to their long-term investment strategy, even during periods of market volatility. A disciplined approach helps avoid impulsive or emotionally driven investment decisions.

Aligning investment goals with risk tolerance enables effective risk management. Investors who understand their risk appetite can construct portfolios that balance risk and potential returns. Investors that diversify across asset classes, industries, and geographies can reduce risk and protect their funds.

Investment goals serve as a benchmark for measuring progress and evaluating the success of investment activities. Regularly reviewing and assessing progress toward goals allows investors to make necessary adjustments to their investment strategy. This iterative process ensures the investment approach remains aligned with evolving circumstances and market conditions.

Setting investment goals empowers individuals to take control of their financial future. By articulating specific objectives and mapping out strategies to achieve them, investors gain a sense of empowerment and independence. Achieving investment goals can provide financial security, freedom, and opportunities for personal and professional growth.

Setting SMART (Specific, Measurable, Achievable, Relevant, Time-bound) goals provides a structured framework for goal setting. Clearly defining the desired outcome, quantifying the target, ensuring achievability, relevance to personal circumstances, and setting a specific timeframe enhances the effectiveness of goal setting.

Investors can assess their risk tolerance through self-reflection, risk profiling questionnaires, or consultations with financial advisors. Evaluating factors such as time horizon, financial goals, past investment experience, and emotional capacity to handle market volatility helps investors gain insights into their risk appetite. This assessment guides asset allocation decisions and the construction of a well-diversified portfolio.

Investment goals and risk tolerance should be reviewed periodically to ensure they remain relevant and aligned with changing circumstances. Life events, financial milestones, or shifts in personal or market conditions may necessitate adjustments to the investment strategy. Regular review and adjustment ensure continued alignment with evolving goals and risk tolerance.

Continuously educating oneself about investment strategies, asset classes, and market trends helps investors make informed decisions. Staying updated with financial news, reading reputable publications, and seeking professional guidance contribute to better investment outcomes.

Observing market dynamics and industry trends facilitates an understanding of market cycles and risk-reward dynamics. Analyzing historical market data and learning from past market cycles helps investors adapt their investment strategy to different market conditions.

Embracing a growth mindset involves embracing challenges, learning from failures, and embracing new opportunities. Investing is a continuous learning process, and adopting a growth mindset fosters resilience, adaptability, and the ability to seize opportunities in the ever-changing cryptocurrency market.

Diversification and portfolio management

Diversification and portfolio management are essential pillars of successful investing, enabling investors to mitigate risk, maximize returns, and navigate the volatile landscape of cryptocurrency markets. Investors can reduce their exposure to particular risks and improve their chances of long-term growth by distributing their assets over a variety of industries, geographies, and asset classes. This section will delve into the significance of diversification and portfolio management in cryptocurrency investing, explore key strategies and considerations, and highlight the benefits of a well-structured portfolio.

Diversification plays a pivotal role in managing risk. Investors reduce exposure to any single investment or sector by spreading investments across various assets. This approach helps mitigate the impact of market volatility and potential losses, preserving capital and enhancing portfolio stability.

Portfolio management aims to optimize risk-adjusted returns. By strategically allocating investments across different assets and market segments, investors can capture upside potential while minimizing the negative impact of underperforming investments. This balanced approach aims to generate consistent, long-term returns.

Diversification and portfolio management aim to preserve capital over time. By constructing a well-diversified portfolio, investors aim to reduce the risk of significant losses that could jeopardize their investment capital. Preservation of capital is fundamental to long-term investment success.

Investors ought to diversify their portfolios among several asset groups, such as equities, bonds, cryptocurrencies, commodities, and real estate. Each asset class has its own risk-return characteristics, and diversifying across them helps reduce the impact of market fluctuations on the overall portfolio.

Investors should diversify within each asset class by allocating investments across different sectors and industries. This approach reduces the concentration risk associated with a single sector's performance. Investing in a variety of sectors provides exposure to different market dynamics and increases the potential for positive returns.

Geographic diversification involves investing in different regions and countries. This strategy spreads exposure to geopolitical and economic risks, reducing the impact of localized events on the portfolio. By accessing global markets, investors can tap into diverse growth opportunities and gain exposure to various currencies and economies.

Portfolio management should consider the investor's time horizon. Short-term goals may require a more conservative approach, while long-term goals can tolerate higher-risk investments. Aligning investment horizons with appropriate asset allocations enhances the effectiveness of portfolio management.

Investors should assess their risk appetite and risk tolerance before constructing a portfolio. Understanding individual comfort levels with volatility and potential losses helps determine the appropriate asset allocation and investment strategy. Risk appetite varies from investor to investor and should be aligned with investment objectives and financial goals.

Regular portfolio rebalancing is crucial to maintain the desired asset allocation and risk-return profile. Rebalancing involves buying or selling assets to realign the portfolio with the target allocation. This strategy helps investors capture gains from outperforming assets and reinvest in underperforming assets, ensuring the portfolio remains in line with their long-term objectives.

Asset allocation is the practice of distributing investments among various asset types. Different asset allocation strategies, such as strategic, tactical, or dynamic allocation, offer varying degrees of risk exposure and potential returns. Investors should select an allocation strategy based on their risk appetite, investment goals, and market outlook.

Regularly monitoring and reviewing the portfolio's performance are crucial for effective portfolio management. Investors should assess the progress towards investment goals, evaluate individual investments' performance, and make necessary adjustments to the portfolio based on changing market conditions and personal circumstances.

Diversification reduces the impact of individual investment risks. Investors reduce the likelihood of suffering substantial losses as a result of a single investment's poor performance by diversifying their investments across a variety of assets and industries. This risk reduction fosters portfolio stability and preserves capital over the long term.

Portfolio management aims to optimize the risk-return tradeoff. By diversifying investments, investors can achieve higher returns for a given level of risk or reduce risk for a desired level of return. Balancing risk and return enhances the overall risk-adjusted performance of the portfolio.

Diversified portfolios provide flexibility and adaptability to changing market conditions. By diversifying across asset classes, sectors, and geographic regions, investors can adjust their portfolio allocations based on market trends and emerging opportunities. This adaptability helps capture potential upside and minimize downside risks.

A well-diversified portfolio provides peace of mind to investors, particularly during turbulent market periods. Knowing that their investments are spread across different assets and sectors reduces anxiety and emotional decision-making. This peace of mind lets investors focus on their long-term investment objectives.

Investors should stay informed about market trends, industry developments, and emerging opportunities. Regular market research and analysis help identify potential investments, assess risk factors, and make informed portfolio management decisions.

Investors should regularly monitor and review their portfolios to remain aligned with investment goals and risk tolerance. Monitoring performance, evaluating individual holdings, and considering market dynamics facilitate timely adjustments and enhancements to the portfolio.

Seeking advice from qualified financial professionals can provide valuable insights and guidance in portfolio management. Financial advisors or investment managers can assist in constructing well-diversified portfolios tailored to individual goals and risk profiles.

Long-term vs. short-term investing approaches

The world of cryptocurrency investing offers many opportunities for investors, with differing strategies based on time horizons. Long-term and short-term investing approaches each come with their unique benefits and considerations. In this section, we will explore the significance of long-term and short-term cryptocurrency investing, discuss the characteristics and strategies associated with each approach, and highlight key considerations to help investors make informed decisions based on their investment goals and risk tolerance.

Long-term investing involves holding assets for an extended period, typically several years or more. This approach focuses on capital appreciation over the long term and emphasizes the fundamental value of investments. Long-term investing is suitable for investors seeking sustainable growth and are willing to tolerate short-term market volatility.

Short-term investing, also known as trading, involves buying and selling assets within a shorter time frame, often ranging from a few hours to several months. This approach aims to capitalize on short-term price fluctuations and focuses on generating quick profits. Short-term investing is suitable for active traders who are comfortable with higher risk levels and adept at technical analysis and market timing.

Long-term investors prioritize the fundamental value of cryptocurrencies. They focus on analyzing the underlying technology, market potential, adoption rate, and the team behind the project. Long-term investing relies on the belief that cryptocurrencies with strong fundamentals will experience sustained growth over time.

Long-term investing requires patience and a willingness to withstand short-term market fluctuations. Investors who adopt this approach understand that the value of cryptocurrencies can fluctuate significantly in the short term but believe in the long-term growth potential of their chosen assets.

The buy-and-hold strategy is a common approach in long-term investing. Investors identify cryptocurrencies with solid fundamentals, accumulate positions over time, and hold onto their investments for an extended period. This strategy aims to capture the potential value appreciation over the long term.

Long-term investors often diversify their portfolios to spread risk across different cryptocurrencies and asset classes. By diversifying, they aim to minimize the impact of any individual investment's performance and capture the growth potential of various cryptocurrencies.

Short-term investors rely heavily on technical analysis to make trading decisions. They analyze price charts, identify trends, and use various indicators to predict short-term price movements. Technical analysis helps traders identify entry and exit points for their trades.

Short-term investors engage in active trading, executing frequent trades based on market trends and price patterns. They aim to capitalize on short-term price fluctuations, buying low and selling high within a relatively short period. Active trading requires monitoring the market closely and reacting swiftly to changing conditions.

Risk management is crucial in short-term investing. Traders set strict stop-loss orders to limit potential losses and use risk management techniques such as position sizing and risk-reward ratios to maximize potential profits. Successful short-term investors emphasize discipline and risk control in their trading strategies.

Scalping involves making multiple trades within a short time frame, aiming to capture small price movements for quick profits. Contrarily, swing trading involves holding positions for a few days to many weeks while taking advantage of short-term price changes. These strategies are common among short-term investors seeking to profit from market volatility.

Investors should assess their risk tolerance before choosing a long-term or short-term approach. Long-term investing typically involves lower levels of risk, as it focuses on fundamental value and is less susceptible to short-term market fluctuations. Short-term investing, however, entails higher risks due to market volatility and requires a higher risk appetite.

Investors should consider their available time and commitment level. Long-term investing requires less active involvement, as investors can hold positions for an extended period. Short-term investing, on the other hand, demands more time and attention, as traders need to monitor the market and execute timely trades closely.

Investors should align their investment goals with the chosen approach. Long-term investing suits those seeking capital appreciation over an extended period, such as retirement planning or wealth accumulation. Short-term investing is suitable for investors looking for quick profits or taking advantage of short-term market opportunities.

The chosen approach should match the investor's knowledge and skills. Long-term investing relies more on fundamental analysis, while short-term investing requires technical analysis and market timing proficiency. Investors should consider their expertise and comfort level with each approach.

Investors should continuously educate themselves about cryptocurrency markets, emerging technologies, and market trends. Staying informed enhances decision-making and allows investors to adapt their strategies based on evolving market conditions.

Observing market dynamics and patterns helps investors identify trends and make informed trading decisions. Regular market analysis and keeping up with news and developments contribute to effective decision-making in both long-term and short-term approaches.

Regardless of the chosen approach, risk management should be a priority. Investors should implement risk management techniques, such as setting stop-loss orders, diversifying portfolios, and managing position sizes. Adhering to risk management principles helps protect capital and maximize potential returns.

Dollar-cost averaging and other investment strategies

Cryptocurrency investing offers unique opportunities for investors seeking to participate in the growing digital asset market. To navigate the volatility and uncertainties, employing effective investment strategies is crucial. Dollar-cost averaging (DCA) and other investment strategies provide frameworks to optimize returns and manage risk. This section will explore the significance of dollar-cost averaging and other investment strategies in cryptocurrency investing, discuss their characteristics and benefits, and highlight key considerations for investors to make informed decisions in their investment journey.

Investing in cryptocurrencies involves inherent market volatility and uncertainty. Dollar-cost averaging and other investment strategies help mitigate timing risk by spreading investments over time, reducing the impact of short-term market fluctuations, and potentially enhancing long-term returns. These strategies provide a systematic and disciplined approach to investing, overcoming emotional decision-making, and maintaining a consistent investment plan. Moreover, they enable investors to balance risk and reward, optimizing the risk-return tradeoff for more effective investment outcomes.

Regardless of market conditions, the investment approach known as dollar-cost averaging (DCA) regularly makes recurring investments of a fixed amount. This approach eliminates the need to time the market perfectly and focuses on accumulating assets gradually over time. By buying fewer shares during periods of high price volatility and more shares during periods of low price volatility, DCA averages out the cost per share over the investment period. The benefits of DCA include risk reduction, disciplined investing, and the potential for a lower average cost per share.

Value investing involves identifying undervalued cryptocurrencies based on fundamental analysis. Investors seek cryptocurrencies with strong technology, a solid development team, and the potential for long-term growth. Value investing aims to capitalize on market inefficiencies and invest at a discounted price. It requires careful research, analysis, and a long-term perspective.

Momentum trading focuses on capitalizing on short-term price trends. Traders identify cryptocurrencies with positive price momentum and enter trades to take advantage of upward price movements. Momentum trading relies on technical analysis indicators and short-term market patterns. This strategy requires active monitoring, quick decision-making, and proficiency in technical analysis.

Growth investing involves investing in cryptocurrencies with high growth potential. Investors look for projects with innovative technology, increasing adoption, and strong market demand. Growth investing aims to generate substantial returns by investing in assets poised for rapid expansion. It requires identifying disruptive projects and assessing their growth prospects.

Contrarian investing involves taking positions opposite to prevailing market sentiment. Investors identify undervalued cryptocurrencies or face negative market sentiment, anticipating a reversal or correction.

Contrarian investing requires contrarian thinking, careful analysis, and the ability to withstand short-term market fluctuations. It can provide opportunities for buying assets at a lower price.

Investors should consider their risk appetite, investment goals, time commitment, and knowledge and skills when selecting an investment strategy. Since some strategies are more conservative and others involve larger degrees of risk, risk appetite is an important factor in choosing the best course of action. Investment goals, whether seeking long-term capital appreciation, short-term gains, or income generation, should align with the chosen strategy. Additionally, time commitment should be evaluated, as some strategies require active involvement and monitoring, while others are more passive in nature. Finally, investors should assess their knowledge and skills, ensuring they have the necessary understanding and expertise to implement the chosen strategy effectively.

Successful cryptocurrency investing requires continuous learning and adaptation. Investors should conduct ongoing market research and analysis to stay informed about cryptocurrency trends, news, and developments. Understanding market dynamics helps investors make informed decisions and adapt their investment strategies to changing conditions. Additionally, effective risk management is critical, and investors should implement risk management techniques such as diversification, stop-loss orders, and position sizing to protect capital and minimize potential losses. Regular evaluation of investment strategies and outcomes allows for adjustments and optimization based on market performance.

CHAPTER VI

Risk Management and Security

Understanding the risks associated with cryptocurrency investing

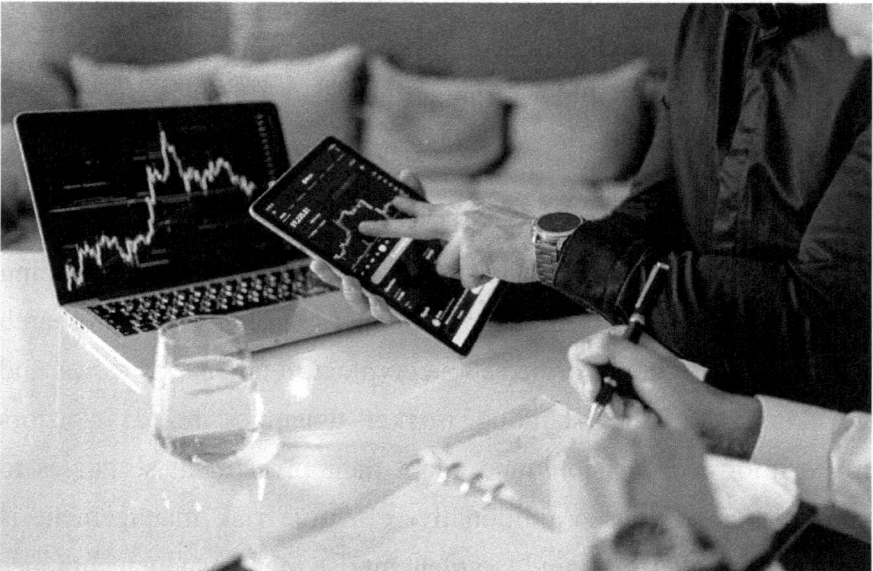

Cryptocurrency investing has gained significant attention recently, attracting seasoned investors and newcomers to the financial world. While the potential for high returns has captivated many, it is essential to understand and address the risks associated with cryptocurrency investments. In this section, we will explore the risks involved in cryptocurrency investing, discuss their impact on investment outcomes, and provide insights into effective risk management strategies to help investors make informed decisions in the dynamic digital asset market.

Extreme price volatility is a characteristic of cryptocurrencies. Rapid price fluctuations can lead to significant gains or losses in short periods, making them susceptible to market speculation, manipulation, and irrational investor behavior.

Cryptocurrency regulations vary significantly across jurisdictions, with governments grappling to define and regulate the rapidly evolving digital asset market. Uncertainty surrounding regulatory frameworks can impact investor confidence and market stability.

The underlying blockchain technology, while revolutionary, is still in its early stages. Technical vulnerabilities, hacking incidents, and software bugs pose risks to the security and integrity of cryptocurrencies, potentially resulting in financial losses for investors.

Cryptocurrencies derive value from factors such as technology, adoption, and market demand. However, their value is primarily driven by speculative investor sentiment, leading to price distortions and increased investment risk.

The volatility of cryptocurrencies exposes investors to the risk of capital loss. Sudden price drops or market downturns can erode investment value, especially for those who need a comprehensive understanding of the risks involved.

Cryptocurrency markets can experience liquidity challenges, particularly for less popular or lower-volume tokens. Illiquid markets make it difficult to execute trades, resulting in potential difficulties in selling or exiting positions when desired.

The decentralized nature of cryptocurrencies introduces security risks. Cyberattacks, hacking incidents, and phishing scams can compromise digital wallets, exchanges, and personal information, leading to financial losses and privacy breaches.

Cryptocurrency investments often involve third-party entities such as exchanges and custodial services. The failure or transgression of these intermediaries can result in the loss or theft of assets, highlighting the importance of choosing reliable and secure service providers.

Thorough research is crucial to understanding the risks associated with specific cryptocurrencies. Before committing capital, investors should evaluate project fundamentals, technology, market demand, and team credibility. Informed decision-making helps mitigate risks associated with investing in volatile and unproven assets.

Diversification is a fundamental risk management strategy. Spreading investments across different cryptocurrencies and other asset classes can reduce exposure to any single investment and balance the overall risk-reward profile of the portfolio.

Setting realistic investment goals based on risk tolerance and time horizons is essential. Investors should align their goals with their risk appetite, understanding that high potential returns come with increased volatility and risk.

Risk mitigation measures such as stop-loss orders, position sizing, and portfolio rebalancing can help protect investments. Setting predetermined exit points and adjusting portfolio allocations based on market conditions are crucial risk management practices.

Security measures for digital wallets are vital to protect cryptocurrencies from theft or unauthorized access. Implementing strong passwords, enabling two-factor authentication, and securely storing wallet information are critical to safeguarding assets.

Cryptocurrency markets are dynamic and ever-changing. Staying informed about market trends, regulatory developments, and emerging risks helps investors make informed decisions and adapt their strategies accordingly.

Investors should assess their risk tolerance and ability to withstand market volatility and potential losses. Understanding personal financial circumstances, goals, and risk appetite helps determine appropriate investment strategies and asset allocations.

Continuous learning about cryptocurrencies, blockchain technology, and market dynamics is essential. Educating oneself about investment principles, risk management strategies, and market trends empowers investors to make informed decisions and adapt to the evolving landscape.

Seeking advice from qualified financial professionals can provide valuable insights and guidance in navigating the risks associated with cryptocurrency investing. Financial advisors or investment managers can help assess risk profiles, develop investment strategies, and provide ongoing support.

Emotional discipline plays a significant role in risk management. Cryptocurrency markets can evoke strong emotions, leading to impulsive decision-making. Investors should remain objective and disciplined, and avoid succumbing to fear or greed when making investment choices.

Implementing risk management techniques

Cryptocurrency investing offers significant opportunities for wealth creation, but it also comes with inherent risks. Implementing effective risk management techniques is paramount to safeguard investments and mitigate potential losses. This section explores the importance of risk management in cryptocurrency investing, discusses key risk management techniques, and provides insights on how investors can protect their capital and enhance the potential for long-term success.

Cryptocurrencies are known for their price volatility and market uncertainties, making risk management crucial for investors. Risk management helps navigate unpredictable conditions and protect investments from adverse market movements. By implementing effective risk management strategies, investors can preserve their capital and maximize risk-adjusted returns.

Diversification is a fundamental risk management technique. Spreading investments across different cryptocurrencies, asset classes, and sectors helps reduce the risk associated with any single investment. It mitigates the impact of adverse market events and enhances the potential for more stable returns.

Position sizing refers to the allocation of capital to individual investments. By determining the appropriate position size for each investment based on risk tolerance and market conditions, investors can manage their exposure to specific cryptocurrencies or assets. This technique helps balance risk across the portfolio.

Stop-loss orders are pre-defined instructions that trigger the sale of an asset when it reaches a specified price level. Implementing stop-loss orders helps limit potential losses by allowing investors to exit a position if the price moves against their expectations. It acts as a safety net during market downturns.

Portfolio rebalancing involves adjusting the allocation of investments in response to market conditions or changes in asset performance. Regularly rebalancing the portfolio helps maintain the desired risk-return profile, ensuring that the portfolio aligns with investment goals and risk tolerance. It prevents overexposure to specific assets or sectors.

Conducting a thorough risk assessment and analysis is essential for effective risk management. Investors should evaluate potential risks associated with specific investments, such as market volatility, regulatory uncertainties, technology risks, and counterparty risks.

This analysis helps make informed decisions and identify appropriate risk management strategies.

Establishing clear investment objectives aligned with financial goals, risk appetite, and time horizon is crucial. Clear objectives serve as a guide for implementing effective risk management techniques and help investors stay focused on their long-term investment plans.

The performance of individual assets, the performance of the portfolio as a whole, and the efficacy of risk management techniques all require constant monitoring of investments. Regular monitoring enables investors to make informed decisions and adjust their approach as necessary.

Learning about cryptocurrency markets, emerging technologies, and regulatory developments is crucial for effective risk management. Staying informed helps investors identify potential risks and adapt their strategies to changing market dynamics. Education empowers investors to make sound decisions.

Emotional discipline plays a vital role in risk management. Cryptocurrency markets can be highly volatile, evoking strong emotions like fear and greed. Investors must remain objective, avoid impulsive decision-making, and adhere to their risk management strategies despite market fluctuations.

Enhancing risk management skills through education, research, and learning from experienced professionals is essential. Developing a deep understanding of risk management principles and techniques empowers investors to make sound decisions and adapt to evolving market conditions.

Investors who lack experience or are uncertain about risk management techniques may benefit from seeking professional advice. Financial advisors or investment managers can provide valuable insights, help assess risk profiles, and offer guidance on implementing effective risk management strategies.

Collaborating with qualified professionals can augment risk management efforts. Financial advisors, legal experts, and technology consultants can provide specialized knowledge and assist investors in understanding complex risks associated with cryptocurrency investing. Their expertise enhances risk management effectiveness.

Dealing with volatility and market fluctuations

The cryptocurrency market is known for its inherent volatility and frequent market fluctuations. While volatility can provide lucrative investment opportunities, it also presents significant challenges for investors. In this section, we will explore the nature of volatility and market fluctuations in the cryptocurrency market, discuss their impact on investment outcomes, and provide insights into effective strategies for dealing with volatility and managing risk in this dynamic environment.

Volatility refers to the rapid and substantial price movements observed in the cryptocurrency market. It is driven by factors such as market sentiment, technological developments, regulatory changes, and macroeconomic events. Volatility creates both opportunities and risks for investors, requiring careful management.

Market fluctuations in the cryptocurrency market result from a combination of factors, including market speculation, supply and demand dynamics changes, investor sentiment, and news events. These fluctuations can be highly unpredictable and impact investment returns significantly.

Volatility in the cryptocurrency market presents opportunities for substantial gains. Rapid price movements can result in significant short-term profits if timed correctly. Investors who embrace volatility and take advantage of price swings may experience significant investment returns.

Volatility also exposes investors to increased risk. Sudden price drops and market downturns can result in significant losses if proper risk management measures are not in place. High volatility requires careful risk assessment and the implementation of strategies to mitigate potential losses.

Market volatility can evoke strong emotions such as fear and greed. Emotional decision-making can lead to impulsive buying at market peaks or panic selling during market downturns. Managing emotions and maintaining a disciplined approach is essential for long-term investment success.

Understanding the nature of volatility in the cryptocurrency market is crucial for setting realistic expectations. Acknowledging that volatility is inherent and that prices can fluctuate rapidly helps investors avoid unrealistic projections and make more informed investment decisions.

Diversification is a fundamental risk management technique that helps reduce the impact of volatility. By spreading investments across different cryptocurrencies, sectors, and asset classes, investors can mitigate the risk associated with any single investment and potentially enhance risk-adjusted returns.

Stop-loss orders are valuable tools for managing risk in volatile markets. Setting predetermined price levels at which to sell an asset can help limit potential losses. Stop-loss orders enable investors to protect their capital by automatically exiting positions if prices reach specified levels.

In order to protect against potential losses caused by negative market fluctuations, hedging procedures entail taking positions. For example, investors can use derivatives such as futures or options to hedge against downside risk. Hedging provides a level of protection in volatile markets.

Volatility in the short term does not necessarily reflect the long-term prospects of cryptocurrencies. Maintaining a long-term perspective helps investors avoid making impulsive decisions based on short-term market fluctuations. Focusing on the underlying technology, adoption potential, and market fundamentals can guide investment decisions.

Investment strategies like dollar-cost averaging can help control volatility. Investors purchase fewer shares during periods of high stock prices and more shares during periods of low stock prices by consistently investing a fixed amount, regardless of market conditions. This strategy reduces the impact of short-term price fluctuations and helps achieve a lower average purchase price over time.

Effective risk management measures are crucial for dealing with volatility. These include diversification, setting stop-loss orders, hedging strategies, and portfolio rebalancing. Implementing these measures helps mitigate potential losses and protect investments during periods of volatility.

Emotional discipline is paramount in managing volatility and market fluctuations. Emotions like fear and greed can lead to impulsive decision-making, often resulting in unfavorable outcomes. Maintaining emotional discipline, sticking to investment strategies, and avoiding reactionary behavior are essential for long-term success.

Continuous education about the cryptocurrency market, emerging technologies, and market dynamics is crucial for navigating volatility. Staying informed helps investors understand the factors driving market fluctuations, identify trends, and make more informed investment decisions.

Investors should regularly assess the effectiveness of their strategies in dealing with volatility. Monitoring investment performance, evaluating risk management techniques, and adjusting strategies based on market conditions enable investors to adapt to changing circumstances and optimize outcomes.

Security best practices for storing and securing cryptocurrencies

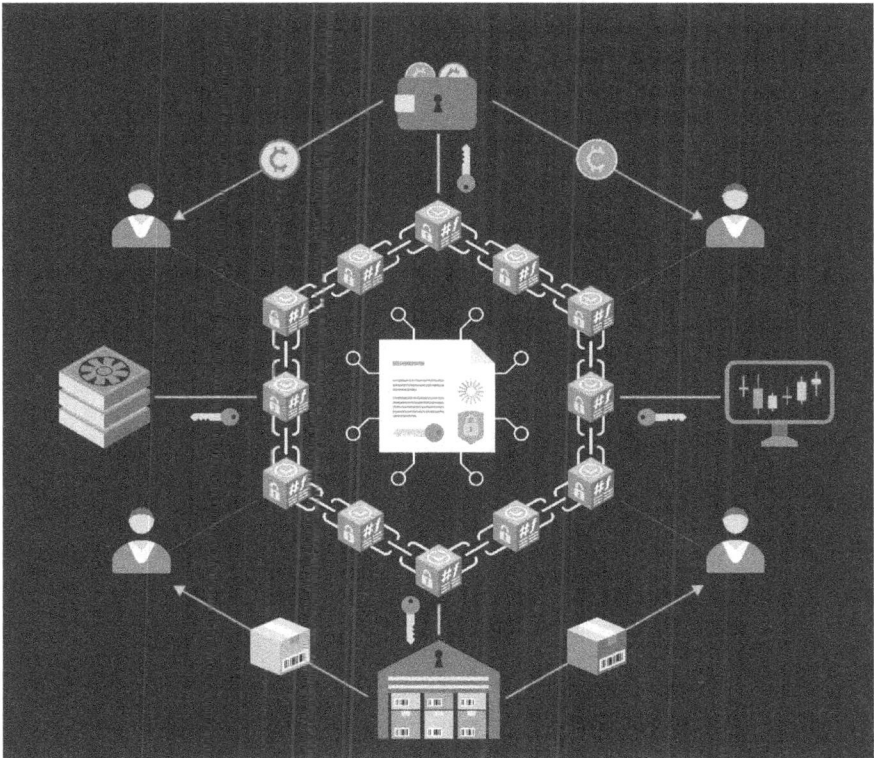

Making sure that digital assets are secure has become essential as the use of cryptocurrencies grows. Cryptocurrencies' decentralized and digital nature necessitates adopting robust security measures to protect against theft, fraud, and hacking. This section will explore security best practices for storing and securing cryptocurrencies, discuss the challenges and risks involved, and provide insights into effective strategies to safeguard your digital assets.

Because they are digital assets that only exist online, cryptocurrencies are susceptible to online threats. Unlike traditional financial systems, cryptocurrencies rely on cryptographic algorithms and decentralized networks, requiring specialized security practices to ensure the safety of funds.

Cryptocurrency transactions, once executed, are generally irreversible. This feature underscores the criticality of maintaining robust security measures to prevent unauthorized access to wallets or the loss of private keys, which can lead to permanent loss of funds.

Cryptocurrencies' decentralized and transparent nature attracts hackers who attempt to exploit vulnerabilities in wallets, exchanges, and other infrastructure. The security of cryptocurrencies is seriously threatened by cyberthreats such phishing scams, malware, and hacking occurrences.

Private keys are crucial for accessing and managing cryptocurrency holdings. Losing or having private keys stolen can result in a permanent loss of funds. Careless storage or insufficient security measures can leave private keys susceptible to theft or loss.

Human error, including unintentional mistakes or falling victim to social engineering tactics, can compromise the security of cryptocurrency holdings. Users may inadvertently reveal private keys or sensitive information, making them vulnerable to attacks.

Hardware wallets are tangible objects made to store private keys offline. They provide an additional layer of security by keeping the keys away from online environments vulnerable to hacking. One of the safest ways to store and secure cryptocurrency is with hardware wallets.

Enabling multi-factor authentication (MFA) adds an extra layer of security to cryptocurrency accounts. Before accessing their accounts, MFA demands users to submit various kinds of identity, such as a password and a distinct verification number sent to their mobile device.

Cold storage refers to storing cryptocurrencies offline, away from internet-connected devices. Methods include paper wallets (physical printouts of private and public keys), offline wallets, and hardware wallets. Cold storage protects against hacking attempts and online vulnerabilities.

Creating strong, unique passwords for cryptocurrency wallets and accounts is vital. Passwords should be lengthy, complex, and contain a combination of letters, numbers, and symbols. Regularly updating passwords and avoiding reuse across platforms enhance security.

Keeping wallet software and operating systems up to date is crucial to protect against known vulnerabilities and security flaws. Developers regularly release updates and patches that address security concerns. Promptly applying these updates ensures the latest security features are in place.

When accessing cryptocurrency accounts or making transactions online, using a secure and trusted internet connection is essential. Public Wi-Fi networks and unsecured connections can expose sensitive information to potential attackers. Utilizing a virtual private network (VPN) adds an extra layer of encryption and security.

Regularly backing up wallet files and ensuring secure storage of backup copies are essential practices. Backups protect against loss or damage to wallets or devices, enabling the recovery of funds in the event of theft, loss, or hardware failure.

Being vigilant and cautious when interacting online helps prevent falling victim to phishing attempts or scams. Verifying website URLs, avoiding suspicious emails, and not sharing sensitive information are critical practices to protect against social engineering attacks.

Maintaining privacy in cryptocurrency transactions is crucial. Utilizing privacy-oriented cryptocurrencies or tools that enhance anonymity, such as privacy-focused wallets or coin mixing services, helps protect against surveillance and potential targeting by malicious actors.

Continuously educating yourself about the evolving security landscape in the cryptocurrency realm is essential. Staying informed about new threats, best practices, and emerging security technologies enables you to make informed decisions and adapt your security measures accordingly.

Engaging with security experts, such as blockchain security firms or professional auditors, can provide invaluable insights into securing your cryptocurrency holdings. These professionals can assess vulnerabilities, provide recommendations, and assist in implementing robust security measures.

Staying informed about legal and regulatory requirements surrounding cryptocurrency security is vital. Understanding the applicable regulations and compliance standards helps ensure adherence to best practices and protects against legal liabilities.

CHAPTER VII

Maximizing Profits in
the Digital Asset Market

Identifying potential investment opportunities

The cryptocurrency market offers many investment opportunities, but identifying the right opportunities requires a comprehensive understanding of market dynamics and careful evaluation. In this section, we will explore the process of identifying potential investment opportunities in the cryptocurrency market, discuss the key factors to consider, and provide insights into effective strategies for maximizing investment potential.

The cryptocurrency market is decentralized and operates 24/7, making it highly dynamic and subject to rapid changes. Understanding the market structure, including market participants, trading volumes, and liquidity, is essential for identifying potential investment opportunities.

The cryptocurrency market is known for its cycles of boom and bust. Recognizing and capitalizing on market trends, such as bull and bear cycles, can help investors identify promising opportunities for both short-term and long-term investments.

Assessing the technological merits of a cryptocurrency project is crucial. Evaluating the underlying blockchain technology, scalability, security features, consensus mechanisms, and unique use cases provides insights into a project's long-term viability and potential.

A cryptocurrency project's success is greatly influenced by the team working on it. Evaluating the expertise, experience, and track record of the team members, including developers, advisors, and founders, helps assess the project's credibility and execution capabilities.

Analyzing market demand and adoption potential is crucial for identifying investment opportunities. Factors such as user base, community engagement, partnerships with established companies, and real-world applications can indicate a cryptocurrency's potential growth and adoption.

Understanding cryptocurrencies' regulatory landscape and compliance requirements in different jurisdictions is essential.

Regulatory clarity and a supportive regulatory environment can significantly impact the growth and acceptance of cryptocurrencies, making them more attractive investment opportunities.

Technical analysis involves studying price trends and chart patterns to identify potential investment opportunities. Analyzing indicators such as support and resistance levels, moving averages, and chart patterns like triangles or double tops can help investors make informed decisions.

Volume analysis provides insights into the strength of buying and selling pressure in the market. High trading volumes during price movements indicate significant market interest and can signal potential investment opportunities.

Analyzing cryptocurrencies' relative strength and momentum compared to the overall market or specific sectors can help identify assets with strong performance potential. Relative strength indicators and momentum oscillators assist in assessing the strength and sustainability of price movements.

News and events are crucial in shaping market sentiment and impacting cryptocurrency prices. Staying informed about industry news, regulatory announcements, technological advancements, and market trends helps investors identify potential investment opportunities and anticipate market movements.

Monitoring social media platforms, online forums, and cryptocurrency communities provides insights into market sentiment. Understanding cryptocurrency sentiment can help investors gauge market expectations and identify potential investment opportunities.

Thorough research is paramount before investing in any cryptocurrency. Investigate the project's whitepaper, technical documentation, team background, and community engagement. Analyze risks associated with technology, market dynamics, regulatory challenges, and competition to make informed investment decisions.

Diversification is a key risk management strategy. Allocating investments across multiple cryptocurrencies and asset classes helps mitigate risks associated with any single investment and enhances the potential for stable returns.

Setting clear investment goals aligned with risk tolerance and time horizons is crucial. Establishing realistic expectations helps manage emotions and allows for a disciplined approach to investing.

Engaging with experienced financial advisors and market analysts can provide valuable insights and guidance in identifying potential investment opportunities. These professionals have in-depth knowledge of cryptocurrency and can offer personalized advice based on individual investment goals.

Accessing market research reports from reputable sources can help investors better understand market trends, project analyses, and potential investment opportunities. These reports provide comprehensive insights into the cryptocurrency landscape.

ICOs, STOs, and other token sales

In the rapidly evolving world of cryptocurrencies, Initial Coin Offerings (ICOs), Security Token Offerings (STOs), and other token sales have emerged as popular fundraising mechanisms. These methods enable projects to raise capital by issuing digital tokens to investors. This section aims to comprehensively understand ICOs, STOs, and other token sales, exploring their nature, benefits, challenges, and regulatory considerations within the cryptocurrency market.

Initial Coin Offerings (ICOs) are fundraising events in which new cryptocurrency projects issue and sell tokens to raise capital. These tokens often represent utility or usage rights within the project's ecosystem. Investors purchase these tokens for future value appreciation or access to project services.

Security Token Offerings (STOs) are token sales that involve the issuance of security tokens, which represent traditional financial instruments such as equity, debt, or profit-sharing rights. Unlike utility tokens offered in ICOs, security tokens are subject to securities regulations and provide investors with legal ownership or rights within the project.

Beyond ICOs and STOs, various other token sale mechanisms exist. Examples include Initial Exchange Offerings (IEOs), Decentralized Finance (DeFi) token sales, and Non-Fungible Token (NFT) sales. These mechanisms offer unique characteristics and serve specific purposes within the cryptocurrency market.

ICOs, STOs, and token sales provide an alternative fundraising avenue, enabling projects to access capital quickly and globally. By leveraging the cryptocurrency community, projects can attract investors from different geographical locations, enhancing their funding opportunities.

Token sales open up investment opportunities to a broader audience, allowing retail investors to participate in early-stage projects traditionally accessible only to venture capitalists or accredited investors. This democratization promotes inclusivity and decentralization within the investment landscape.

Tokens issued in ICOs, STOs, and other token sales often have the potential for liquidity in secondary markets. This liquidity can allow investors to trade and realize returns on their investments, enhancing market efficiency and investor exit options.

Token sales incentivize early adopters and investors to participate in the project's ecosystem. This creates network effects, where the token's value and the project's ecosystem increase as the user base grows. Token holders may gain access to exclusive project services or benefits, fostering community engagement and ecosystem expansion.

The cryptocurrency sector is still in its early stages, and different countries have different laws governing ICOs, STOs, and token sales. This lack of regulatory clarity exposes investors to potential risks, such as fraudulent projects, inadequate disclosure, and the absence of investor protection mechanisms.

The cryptocurrency market's inherent volatility poses risks for token sale participants. Fluctuations in token prices can result in significant gains or losses. Investors must carefully assess the market dynamics, project fundamentals, and risk-reward profiles before participating in token sales.

Token sales often rely on blockchain technology, which may face technical challenges, including scalability limitations, network congestion, and smart contract vulnerabilities. Additionally, funds and personal information security can be compromised by cyber threats, hacking incidents, or fraudulent activities.

Not all projects that conduct token sales possess the necessary technical expertise, market understanding, or viable business models. Investing in projects with inadequate planning, poor execution, or unrealistic promises can result in lost invested funds.

STOs and certain token sales are subject to securities regulations in various jurisdictions. Complying with securities laws, including registration, disclosure, and investor accreditation requirements, is crucial for projects issuing security tokens to ensure legal compliance and investor protection.

Regulatory frameworks often mandate Anti-Money Laundering (AML) and Know Your Customer (KYC) procedures to prevent money laundering, terrorist financing, and fraud. Token sales may need to implement robust AML and KYC measures to verify the identity of participants and ensure compliance with relevant regulations.

Regulatory frameworks surrounding ICOs, STOs, and token sales are continuously evolving. Monitoring regulatory developments and seeking legal advice is essential to navigate changing compliance requirements and ensure adherence to applicable laws.

Investors must conduct comprehensive due diligence on projects before participating in token sales. This involves evaluating the project's whitepaper, team background, technology roadmap, market viability, and legal compliance. Assessing project fundamentals and conducting independent research mitigate investment risks.

Diversifying investments across different projects reduces exposure to any single project's risks. Allocating capital to a portfolio of well-researched projects with diverse use cases, teams, and industries improves the potential for stable returns and risk mitigation.

Seeking advice from qualified professionals, such as financial advisors, legal experts, or blockchain consultants, provides valuable insights and guidance in assessing token sale opportunities. These professionals can assist in evaluating projects, navigating regulatory complexities, and identifying potential risks.

Yield farming, staking, and other passive income strategies

The cryptocurrency market not only offers opportunities for capital appreciation but also provides avenues for earning passive income. Yield farming, staking, and other passive income strategies have gained popularity among cryptocurrency investors seeking to generate returns through their digital asset holdings. This section will explore these strategies, their benefits, risks, and the evolving landscape of passive income opportunities in cryptocurrency.

Yield farming involves leveraging decentralized finance (DeFi) platforms to earn returns on cryptocurrency holdings. Participants provide liquidity to liquidity pools and, in return, receive rewards through additional tokens or fees generated by the protocol.

Staking is the process of holding and "staking" specific cryptocurrencies in a blockchain network to support network operations and secure the network. In return for participating in the network consensus, stakers receive rewards through additional tokens or transaction fees.

Beyond yield farming and staking, various other passive income strategies exist in the cryptocurrency market. These include lending and borrowing platforms, masternode hosting, liquidity provision in decentralized exchanges, and participation in tokenized real estate or dividend-paying token projects.

Passive income strategies in the cryptocurrency market offer the potential for attractive returns. By participating in yield farming, staking, or other passive income strategies, investors can earn rewards through additional tokens, fees, or interest, augmenting their overall investment returns.

Engaging in passive income strategies allows investors to diversify their cryptocurrency holdings beyond pure capital appreciation. By earning rewards or interest through these strategies, investors can mitigate the risk associated with holding a single cryptocurrency and benefit from a broader portfolio exposure.

Participating in yield farming or providing liquidity to decentralized exchanges contributes to the liquidity and efficiency of the cryptocurrency market. Passive income strategies help promote the growth and stability of the overall ecosystem.

The cryptocurrency market is known for its volatility, which can impact the returns generated through passive income strategies. Fluctuations in token prices can affect the value of rewards, and investors must be prepared for potential decreases in the value of their holdings.

Many passive income strategies rely on smart contracts, which are susceptible to vulnerabilities and coding errors. Smart contract risks include bugs, hacking attempts, or exploits that can lead to financial losses. Proper due diligence and choosing reputable platforms are essential to mitigate these risks.

Yield farming and liquidity provision strategies expose participants to the risk of impermanent loss. Impermanent loss occurs when the value of assets held in a liquidity pool fluctuates compared to holding the assets separately. Understanding and managing this risk is crucial when engaging in these strategies.

The cryptocurrency market's regulatory environment for passive income strategies is still evolving. Participants must be aware of potential legal and compliance risks associated with the platforms they use. Additionally, platform risks, such as hacks, security breaches, or fraudulent projects, pose challenges that require careful selection of reputable platforms.

The DeFi ecosystem continues to innovate, providing new passive income opportunities. New protocols, yield aggregators, and decentralized lending platforms emerge, offering novel ways to generate returns on cryptocurrency holdings. Staying informed about these developments is crucial to capitalize on emerging opportunities.

The tokenization of assets, such as real estate or dividend-paying stocks, creates opportunities for earning passive income. Tokenized projects allow investors to benefit from the income generated by these assets, offering exposure to traditional markets through the cryptocurrency ecosystem.

The transition to Proof-of-Stake (PoS) consensus mechanisms in various blockchain networks opens doors for staking and earning rewards. As more projects adopt PoS, investors can explore additional staking opportunities beyond well-established networks like Ethereum.

Thoroughly researching platforms, protocols, and projects is essential before participating in passive income strategies. Conducting due diligence on the technology, team, security measures, and user feedback helps identify reputable and trustworthy platforms.

Diversifying investments across different passive income strategies, cryptocurrencies, and platforms mitigates risks associated with a single investment. Allocating assets based on risk tolerance, expected returns, and project fundamentals helps optimize risk-reward profiles.

Regularly assessing the risks associated with passive income strategies, staying informed about market developments, and actively monitoring platform security and performance are essential practices. Setting realistic expectations and preparing for potential market volatility enhance risk management efforts.

Active participation in cryptocurrency communities, forums, and social media platforms provides valuable insights and knowledge sharing. Engaging with experienced participants helps navigate the landscape, gain insights, and identify reputable platforms.

Taking advantage of market trends and timing

The cryptocurrency market is known for its dynamic nature, characterized by rapid price movements and market trends. Understanding and effectively capitalizing on market trends and timing is crucial for investors seeking to maximize their returns. In this section, we will explore the concept of market trends, discuss the significance of timing in cryptocurrency investing, and provide insights into strategies for identifying and taking advantage of market trends.

Market trends describe the general direction that a specific cryptocurrency or the market as a whole is moving. Trends can be classified as bullish (upward), bearish (downward), or sideways (horizontal). Recognizing and analyzing these trends helps investors make informed decisions about their investment strategies.

Market trends in the cryptocurrency market are influenced by various factors, including technological developments, regulatory news, macroeconomic events, investor sentiment, and market adoption. These factors can drive price movements and create opportunities for investors.

Timing plays a critical role in cryptocurrency investing. Buying or selling assets at the right time can lead to substantial profits, while poor timing can result in losses or missed opportunities. Identifying optimal entry and exit points within market trends is key to maximizing investment returns.

Timing the market is inherently challenging due to its unpredictable nature. Factors such as market volatility, sudden price movements, and the influence of external events make it difficult to predict the timing of market shifts accurately. However, investors can employ strategies to increase their chances of success.

Technical analysis involves studying historical price data, chart patterns, and trading indicators to identify market trends and potential price movements. Analyzing indicators such as moving averages, relative strength index (RSI), and trend lines can provide insights into market direction.

Fundamental analysis' primary objective is to evaluate the intrinsic value and potential of cryptocurrencies. Assessing factors such as technology, team, partnerships, market demand, and adoption potential helps investors identify cryptocurrencies with strong fundamentals and growth potential.

Monitoring news and market sentiment can provide insights into current trends and potential future price movements. Staying informed about industry developments, regulatory announcements, and significant events helps investors gauge market sentiment and adjust their strategies accordingly.

Trend following involves identifying and investing in assets that are in established uptrends. Investors aim to ride the momentum of a trend, buying when prices are rising and selling when the trend shows signs of reversal. Trend-following strategies often employ technical indicators and stop-loss orders for risk management.

Contrarian investing involves taking positions that go against prevailing market sentiment. Contrarians believe that markets tend to overreact to news and events, presenting opportunities for profitable trades. Contrarian strategies require careful analysis of market sentiment and identifying potential reversals in trends.

Regardless of the state of the market, investors who use the dollar-cost averaging technique regularly make regular, fixed-amount investments. By investing at predetermined intervals, investors buy more when prices are low and less when prices are high. This strategy minimizes the impact of short-term market volatility and allows for long-term accumulation of assets.

Effective risk management is essential when taking advantage of market trends. Setting stop-loss orders, diversifying investments, and establishing a risk tolerance are crucial to protect against potential losses and manage portfolio volatility.

Investors often fall victim to emotional biases, such as fear of missing out (FOMO) or fear of loss, which can cloud judgment and lead to impulsive decisions. Overcoming these biases and maintaining emotional discipline is crucial for successful trend analysis and timing.

Successful trend analysis requires patience and a long-term perspective. It is essential to distinguish short-term price fluctuations from long-term trends. Investors who can stay focused on the big picture and resist the temptation to chase short-term gains are more likely to make sound investment decisions.

Market trends are not static and can change rapidly. Investors must regularly monitor and analyze market conditions, trends, and indicators to stay informed and adapt their strategies accordingly.

Being flexible and adaptable is vital in the cryptocurrency market. Trends can shift quickly, and investors must be prepared to adjust their strategies, and entry or exit points, or even change investment positions based on new information or changing market conditions.

CHAPTER VIII

Overcoming Common Challenges in Cryptocurrency Investing

Dealing with FUD (Fear, Uncertainty, and Doubt)

The cryptocurrency market is inherently volatile and has various emotional challenges, including fear, uncertainty, and doubt (FUD). FUD can significantly impact investor decision-making and lead to impulsive actions or missed opportunities. In this section, we will explore the concept of FUD and its effects on the cryptocurrency market. We will also provide insights and strategies for effectively dealing with FUD to make informed investment decisions.

FUD refers to the spread of negative sentiments, rumors, or misinformation aimed at creating fear, uncertainty, and doubt among market participants. FUD can originate from various sources, including media coverage, social media platforms, regulatory announcements, or market manipulation attempts.

FUD triggers emotional responses in investors, such as panic selling, hesitancy to invest, or loss of confidence in the market. These emotional responses can lead to irrational decision-making, increased market volatility, and missed opportunities for investors.

Media outlets often sensationalize negative news related to cryptocurrencies, focusing on potential risks, scandals, or market downturns. This coverage can amplify FUD and create a biased perception of the cryptocurrency market.

FUD may spread quickly on social media sites and online discussion boards. False rumors, unverified claims, and manipulation attempts can quickly circulate, affecting investor sentiment and market dynamics.

Regulatory announcements and government actions can instill uncertainty and doubt in the cryptocurrency market. Changes in regulations, bans, or investigations into fraudulent activities can trigger FUD among investors.

FUD often triggers emotional biases, such as fear of missing out (FOMO) or fear of loss, leading to panic selling. Investors may make impulsive decisions based on short-term market fluctuations, disregarding long-term fundamentals.

FUD can cause investors to miss out on potential opportunities. In times of market uncertainty, valuable projects may experience temporary price drops, presenting buying opportunities that fearful investors might overlook.

Heightened FUD can increase market volatility, as panic-driven buying or selling can amplify price swings. Manipulative actors may exploit this volatility to influence market movements for personal gain.

Understanding the fundamentals of cryptocurrencies and the underlying technology is crucial for overcoming FUD. Educating oneself through reliable sources and conducting thorough research enables investors to make informed decisions based on knowledge rather than emotion.

Developing critical thinking skills helps investors evaluate information objectively. Assessing the credibility and validity of news, rumors, or claims reduces the impact of FUD on decision-making processes.

Maintaining a long-term perspective is essential when dealing with FUD. Recognizing that cryptocurrency markets are prone to short-term volatility and focusing on the long-term potential and investment fundamentals can mitigate FUD's effects.

Diversifying investments across different cryptocurrencies, sectors, or asset classes helps spread risk and reduces vulnerability to FUD in specific projects. Diversification provides a buffer against negative market events and allows for exposure to various opportunities.

Implementing risk management strategies, such as setting stop-loss orders, establishing an investment plan aligned with risk tolerance, and maintaining a diversified portfolio, helps manage potential losses and protects against impulsive decision-making driven by FUD.

Being selective in the information consumed and the sources trusted can help filter out FUD. Relying on reputable news outlets, verified data sources, and credible community discussions reduces exposure to misinformation and reduces the impact of FUD on investor sentiment.

Recognizing and understanding one's emotional responses to FUD is crucial. Being aware of fear, uncertainty, or doubt allows investors to take a step back, evaluate information objectively, and make rational decisions based on facts rather than emotions.

Developing emotional discipline involves controlling impulsive reactions to FUD and adhering to investment strategies and plans. Setting clear goals, establishing investment rules, and avoiding knee-jerk reactions based on short-term market movements promote disciplined decision-making.

Engaging with financial advisors, cryptocurrency experts, or investment professionals can provide valuable guidance and support in navigating FUD. Professionals can provide a broader perspective, offer insights into market trends, and help manage emotional challenges.

Participating in cryptocurrency communities, forums, or social media groups allows investors to share experiences, gain insights, and obtain emotional support from like-minded individuals. Collaborative discussions and knowledge sharing can help counteract the effects of FUD.

Seeking mentorship from experienced investors or joining investment groups can provide guidance and support in dealing with FUD. Learning from those who have successfully navigated market uncertainties can help build resilience and enhance decision-making abilities.

Handling emotional biases and avoiding herd mentality

Emotions play a significant role in investment decision-making, particularly in the dynamic and volatile cryptocurrency market. Emotional biases and the tendency to follow the herd can cloud judgment, leading to irrational choices and potentially detrimental outcomes. This section explores the impact of emotional biases and herd mentality in the cryptocurrency market and provides strategies for handling these biases to make rational investment decisions.

Emotional biases refer to systematic errors in judgment and decision-making driven by emotions. Several types of emotional biases can influence investor behavior, including fear of missing out (FOMO), loss aversion, confirmation bias, and overconfidence bias. These biases can lead to distorted perceptions and flawed decision-making processes.

Psychological factors, such as the need for certainty, fear of loss, and the influence of social proof, contribute to the formation of emotional biases. Understanding these underlying psychological mechanisms is crucial for effectively addressing and managing emotional biases.

Investors frequently make rash decisions because they are afraid of missing out on possible gains due to FOMO (Fear of Missing Out). It can lead to entering the market at inflated prices or investing in speculative projects without conducting thorough research.

Loss aversion is the propensity to favor preventing losses over achieving benefits. Investors may hold onto losing positions longer than necessary or sell winning positions prematurely to avoid further losses, which can impact portfolio performance.

Confirmation bias occurs when investors seek information that confirms their pre-existing beliefs or biases while disregarding contradictory evidence. This bias can lead to the selective interpretation of information and hinder objective analysis.

Overconfidence bias manifests as an unwarranted belief in one's abilities and the accuracy of predictions. Investors may underestimate risks, overestimate their abilities to time the market, or make excessive trades driven by misplaced confidence.

Developing self-awareness and reflecting on emotional biases are essential first steps. Recognizing the presence of biases and understanding how they influence decision-making enable investors to make more objective and rational choices.

Educating oneself about cryptocurrencies, investment principles, and market dynamics helps reduce emotional biases. Gathering reliable information, understanding fundamental analysis, and conducting thorough research foster a more informed investment approach.

Diversifying investments across different cryptocurrencies, sectors, and asset classes reduces the impact of emotional biases on a single investment. By spreading risk, investors can avoid excessive emotional attachment to specific assets and maintain a balanced portfolio.

Maintaining a long-term perspective helps mitigate the impact of short-term emotional biases. Recognizing that the cryptocurrency market is volatile and subject to fluctuations allows investors to focus on the potential long-term value of their investments.

Implementing risk management strategies, such as setting stop-loss orders, establishing risk tolerance levels, and diversifying investments, helps manage emotional biases related to fear and loss aversion. Adopting a disciplined approach to risk management fosters rational decision-making.

Actively seeking out contrarian views and diverse opinions challenges confirmation bias. Engaging with individuals with different perspectives can provide valuable insights, broaden perspectives, and help investors avoid the trap of biased thinking.

Herd mentality refers to individuals' tendency to follow the majority's actions and decisions. In the cryptocurrency market, herd mentality can lead to the adoption of popular opinions or investment trends without conducting independent analysis.

Herd mentality can amplify market volatility, resulting in inflated asset prices driven by irrational exuberance. It can also lead to market bubbles, where asset prices become detached from their intrinsic value.

Encouraging independent thinking is crucial for avoiding herd mentality. Investors should analyze information critically, consider multiple perspectives, and conduct their own research before making investment decisions.

Contrarian investing involves going against the crowd and taking positions that deviate from prevailing market sentiment. Adopting a contrarian approach allows investors to identify undervalued assets and capitalize on market inefficiencies.

Developing a well-reasoned investment thesis based on fundamental analysis and independent research provides a solid foundation for investment decisions. Following thorough analysis rather than popular opinions helps investors avoid herd mentality.

Establishing clear investment goals aligned with individual risk tolerance and financial objectives helps anchor decision-making. Defining specific goals provides a framework for rational choices and reduces the impact of emotional biases.

Rational decision-making involves assessing facts objectively, considering both positive and negative aspects, and weighing risks and rewards. Embracing rational processes allows investors to make informed decisions based on data and analysis.

Emotional detachment involves separating emotions from investment decisions. Developing a disciplined mindset, focusing on objective criteria, and avoiding impulsive actions driven by emotions promote rational decision-making.

Engaging with financial advisors, investment professionals, or cryptocurrency experts can provide valuable guidance and support in managing emotional biases and avoiding herd mentality. Professional advice helps ensure a balanced and rational investment approach.

Learning from past market crashes and corrections

The cryptocurrency market has experienced numerous crashes and corrections throughout history, with significant price declines and market volatility. While these downturns can be unsettling for investors, they also present valuable opportunities for learning and growth. This section explores the lessons that can be derived from past market crashes and corrections in the cryptocurrency market. Investors can develop a resilient investment approach that navigates market downturns with greater confidence by analyzing historical events, identifying common patterns, and understanding the underlying factors.

Market crashes and corrections are periods of significant price declines and market volatility. Crashes refer to rapid and severe price declines, often accompanied by panic selling and a loss of investor confidence. Conversely, corrections are more moderate price declines that occur after periods of rapid market growth, serving as a healthy adjustment to market conditions.

Various factors contribute to market crashes and corrections, including market speculation, regulatory developments, technological vulnerabilities, macroeconomic events, and investor sentiment. Understanding these underlying causes is crucial for comprehending the dynamics of market downturns.

Examining the early years of the cryptocurrency market reveals notable crashes, such as the Mt. Gox collapse in 2014 and the Ethereum flash crash in 2017. These events exposed vulnerabilities in exchanges and highlighted the need for improved security measures and regulatory oversight.

The 2017-2018 period, we witnessed an unprecedented surge in cryptocurrency prices, followed by a significant market correction. The bubble burst, and prices experienced a sharp decline. Factors such as speculative investment behavior, initial coin offering (ICO) hype, and regulatory concerns contributed to the market's volatility.

The outbreak of the COVID-19 pandemic in 2020 triggered a global economic downturn, affecting various asset classes, including cryptocurrencies. The market experienced a significant correction, followed by a recovery driven by increasing institutional interest and adoption.

Market downturns underscore the significance of implementing effective risk management strategies. Setting stop-loss orders, diversifying portfolios, and maintaining an emergency fund can help mitigate potential losses and preserve long-term investment objectives.

Examining past market cycles reveals the cyclical nature of the cryptocurrency market. Recognizing that market downturns are part of the broader market cycle allows investors to maintain a long-term perspective and avoid reactionary decision-making.

Market crashes and corrections present opportunities for investors with a long-term investment horizon. Buying assets at discounted prices during market downturns can yield substantial returns when the market recovers. Identifying undervalued projects with strong fundamentals is crucial during these periods.

Past market crashes highlight the importance of emotional discipline in investment decision-making. Emotional biases like panic selling or FOMO-driven buying can lead to suboptimal outcomes. Cultivating emotional resilience and adhering to investment plans can help investors navigate market downturns effectively.

The cryptocurrency market has been significantly influenced by recent advancements in regulatory frameworks. Past crashes emphasize the importance of staying informed about regulatory changes and complying with legal requirements. Adhering to regulations helps build trust in the market and protects investors from potential risks.

Market crashes and corrections provide valuable learning experiences for investors. Studying the underlying causes, analyzing market trends, and staying updated on industry developments are essential for adapting investment strategies to changing market conditions.

Thorough research and due diligence are essential for identifying quality projects and understanding their potential risks. Evaluating project fundamentals, team expertise, market demand, and competition helps investors make informed decisions and build resilient portfolios.

Diversifying investments across different cryptocurrencies, sectors, and asset classes helps mitigate risk and minimize the impact of individual market crashes. Allocating investments based on risk tolerance and diversifying across established and emerging projects can enhance portfolio resilience.

Maintaining realistic expectations about potential returns and market volatility is crucial. Recognizing that the cryptocurrency market is highly speculative and subject to significant fluctuations helps investors avoid irrational expectations and react calmly during market downturns.

Actively participating in cryptocurrency communities, forums, and social media groups provides valuable insights and knowledge sharing. Engaging with experienced investors and industry experts facilitates the exchange of ideas, strategies, and perspectives, strengthening decision-making abilities.

Regularly assessing the performance and composition of investment portfolios allows investors to identify potential risks and make adjustments accordingly. Rebalancing portfolios based on changing market conditions helps maintain an optimal risk-reward balance.

Strategies for staying updated with market news and trends

The cryptocurrency market is characterized by its dynamic nature, with constant innovations, regulatory developments, and market trends shaping the industry. Staying updated with market news and trends is essential for investors seeking to make informed decisions and adapt to the evolving landscape. This section explores strategies for staying abreast of market news and trends in the cryptocurrency industry. By employing these strategies, investors can enhance their knowledge, identify emerging opportunities, and navigate the fast-paced world of cryptocurrencies.

The cryptocurrency market experiences rapid changes, including new projects, technological advancements, and regulatory updates. Staying updated allows investors to understand the latest developments and their potential impact on the market.

Market trends and investor sentiment play a crucial role in cryptocurrency investing. Awareness of emerging trends helps investors identify opportunities, make informed decisions, and manage risks effectively.

The regulatory landscape surrounding cryptocurrencies is continuously evolving. Keeping up with regulatory changes and legal developments helps investors navigate compliance requirements and mitigate potential risks.

Accessing reliable news sources and aggregators specialized in cryptocurrency news is essential. Reputable platforms provide up-to-date information, market analysis, and insights into the latest trends, helping investors make informed decisions.

Following influential figures and thought leaders in the cryptocurrency industry can provide valuable insights and expert opinions. Subscribing to their blogs, social media accounts, or podcasts enables investors to access their perspectives on market trends and emerging projects.

Participating in cryptocurrency communities and forums facilitates knowledge sharing and idea exchange. Engaging with like-minded individuals lets investors stay updated with community discussions, emerging projects, and market insights.

Attending cryptocurrency conferences and events provides opportunities to learn from industry experts, network with professionals, and gain insights into the latest market trends.

Conferences often feature keynote speeches, panel discussions, and workshops on diverse topics relevant to the cryptocurrency industry.

Monitoring social media platforms like Twitter, Reddit, and Telegram can provide real-time updates on market news, project announcements, and investor sentiment. Engaging with cryptocurrency communities on these platforms enables investors to stay connected and informed.

Subscribing to newsletters and research reports from reputable sources offers a consolidated and curated stream of market news and trends. These resources often provide in-depth analysis, market research, and expert opinions, helping investors comprehensively understand the industry.

Leveraging cryptocurrency price and data platforms provide investors with real-time market data, price charts, and indicators. These platforms offer insights into price movements, trading volumes, and market capitalization, helping investors track market trends and identify potential investment opportunities.

With vast information available, filtering relevant and reliable information is crucial. Developing critical thinking skills helps investors discern valuable insights from noise and misinformation, ensuring they make well-informed decisions.

Information overload can lead to decision paralysis and emotional biases. Setting limits on information consumption allows investors to maintain focus and prevent being overwhelmed by constant updates. Establishing a routine for the consumption of information helps create a balance between the need to be informed and the desire to avoid becoming overwhelmed with information.

Using technology and tools such as news aggregators, data analytics platforms, and content curation tools can streamline the process of staying updated. These tools can help filter information, provide personalized news feeds, and offer customized alerts based on specific interests and preferences.

Continuous learning and self-study are vital for staying updated in the cryptocurrency market. Learning about market dynamics, fundamental analysis, technical analysis, and blockchain technology improves one's capacity to identify market trends and make wise investment choices.

Dedicating time to research emerging projects, technologies, and blockchain use cases allows investors to identify potential opportunities early on. Investigating project whitepapers, team backgrounds, partnerships, and community engagement provides valuable insights into the viability and potential of projects.

Analyzing market data and indicators helps investors understand market trends and sentiment. Investors can see patterns, levels of support and resistance, and future market reversals using technical analysis tools including moving averages, RSI, and trend lines.

The cryptocurrency market is constantly evolving, and strategies must be adaptable to changing market dynamics. Being open to adjusting investment strategies, entry and exit points, and risk management approaches based on new information and market conditions is crucial for long-term success.

Staying updated with market news and trends involves evaluating risk and reward potential. Investors must assess the potential risks associated with emerging projects, regulatory developments, and market trends, while also considering the potential rewards offered by innovative technologies and market opportunities.

Regularly monitoring and adjusting investment portfolios based on changing market trends and information is vital. Rebalancing portfolios, reallocating assets, and incorporating new investment opportunities ensure alignment with investment goals and market conditions.

CHAPTER IX

The Future of
Cryptocurrency Investing

Trends and developments in the cryptocurrency industry

The cryptocurrency industry has experienced rapid growth and evolution since the inception of Bitcoin in 2009. Over the years, numerous trends and developments have shaped the industry, impacting its technology, market dynamics, and regulatory landscape. This section explores the significant trends and developments in the cryptocurrency industry. By examining key areas such as blockchain technology, decentralized finance (DeFi), institutional adoption, regulatory advancements, and sustainability initiatives, we gain insights into the current state of the industry and its future prospects.

As the demand for blockchain technology grows, scalability remains a critical challenge. Innovations such as layer-two solutions (e.g., Lightning Network) and sharding aim to improve scalability by increasing transaction throughput and reducing fees, fostering wider adoption.

Interoperability between different blockchain networks has become a focus, aiming to enable seamless communication and asset transfers. Projects like Polkadot and Cosmos are building frameworks to facilitate interoperability, fostering collaboration and the growth of decentralized applications (dApps).

Privacy has gained importance in the cryptocurrency industry. Privacy-focused cryptocurrencies like Monero and Zcash utilize advanced cryptographic techniques to ensure secure and confidential transactions. Privacy solutions are becoming increasingly integrated into blockchain protocols to protect user data.

Decentralized Exchanges (DEXs), such as Uniswap and SushiSwap, have gained popularity, allowing users to trade cryptocurrencies directly from their wallets without intermediaries. DEXs promote financial inclusivity, liquidity provision, and transparency in the trading process.

Automated Market Makers (AMMs) are a crucial component of DeFi, enabling decentralized trading and liquidity provision. Protocols like Balancer and Curve employ AMMs to facilitate asset swaps and provide efficient price discovery mechanisms.

As a new trend, yield farming enables users to profit by supplying liquidity to DeFi protocols. Liquidity mining incentivizes participation and drives capital flows into DeFi applications, promoting network growth and decentralized governance.

Institutions, including banks, hedge funds, and corporations, increasingly recognize the potential of cryptocurrencies as an asset class. High-profile investments by companies like Tesla and institutional adoption of Bitcoin as a store of value demonstrate growing confidence in the industry.

Traditional financial institutions are building infrastructure to support cryptocurrency transactions. This includes custodial services, institutional-grade trading platforms, and regulatory-compliant investment products, improving accessibility and trust for institutional investors.

Regulatory authorities are providing more precise guidelines for cryptocurrency operations. Regulatory frameworks like the European Union's Markets in Crypto-Assets (MiCA) and the United States proposed Crypto-Currency Act aim to establish a transparent and secure regulatory environment.

Governments and regulatory bodies are increasingly recognizing the potential of digital assets. Countries like Switzerland, Singapore, and Malta have implemented favorable regulations to attract cryptocurrency businesses and foster innovation.

Regulators are focusing on enhancing investor protection measures. This includes measures such as Know Your Customer (KYC) and Anti-Money Laundering (AML) requirements and licensing and compliance standards for cryptocurrency exchanges and service providers.

Central banks worldwide are exploring the concept of Central Bank Digital Currencies (CBDCs), digital versions of fiat currencies. Projects like China's Digital Currency Electronic Payment (DCEP) and the European Central Bank's investigation into a digital euro signify the potential for digital currencies to reshape monetary systems.

The environmental impact of cryptocurrencies has gained attention. Proof-of-Stake (PoS) consensus algorithms, used by projects like Cardano and Ethereum 2.0, aim to reduce energy consumption and carbon footprints compared to the energy-intensive Proof-of-Work (PoW) algorithm.

Cryptocurrency projects are exploring initiatives to offset carbon emissions and promote eco-friendly practices. Green mining initiatives leverage renewable energy sources to power mining operations, reducing reliance on fossil fuels.

Environmental, Social, and Governance (ESG) factors are increasingly important for investors. Cryptocurrency projects incorporate ESG principles into their frameworks, ensuring transparency, ethical practices, and social responsibility.

Potential regulatory changes and their impact

The cryptocurrency industry operates within a regulatory landscape that continues to evolve and adapt to the unique challenges posed by digital assets. As cryptocurrencies gain widespread adoption and the market matures, regulators worldwide are considering new frameworks to address concerns regarding investor protection, financial stability, and anti-money laundering measures. This section explores potential regulatory changes and their impact on the cryptocurrency industry. By analyzing key areas such as regulatory frameworks, compliance requirements, taxation, and global cooperation, we gain insights into the potential trajectory of regulations and their implications for market participants.

Regulatory frameworks aim to protect investors by establishing standards for market participants, disclosure requirements, and anti-fraud measures. Regulations help promote transparency, mitigate risks, and instill confidence in the cryptocurrency market.

Regulatory oversight addresses concerns related to financial stability by implementing measures to prevent market manipulation, enhance transparency, and promote responsible financial practices within the cryptocurrency industry.

Regulations combat illicit activities by imposing AML and KYC requirements on cryptocurrency exchanges and service providers. These measures help prevent money laundering, terrorist financing, and other illegal activities.

Commodity Futures Trading Commission also known as CFTC and the Securities and Exchange Commission also known as SEC, each regulate different facets of the cryptocurrency business, as part of the United States' comprehensive approach to regulation. Potential regulatory changes include more precise definitions of cryptocurrencies, enhanced investor protection, and improved regulatory coordination.

The European Union has introduced the Markets in Crypto-Assets (MiCA) proposal to establish a comprehensive regulatory framework for cryptocurrencies. MiCA seeks to harmonize regulations across member states, enhance investor protection, and address market integrity concerns.

Countries in the Asia-Pacific region have adopted diverse approaches to cryptocurrency regulation. Japan has implemented a licensing regime for cryptocurrency exchanges, while South Korea focuses on AML measures. China has taken a strict stance on cryptocurrency trading and initial coin offerings (ICOs), while countries like Singapore embrace a more supportive regulatory environment to foster innovation.

International bodies, like Financial Action Task Force (FATF), are working towards establishing consistent AML and KYC standards for cryptocurrencies. Collaborative efforts promote regulatory harmonization, reduce regulatory arbitrage, and enhance global compliance.

Stricter compliance requirements, such as AML and KYC procedures, impose additional costs and operational burdens on cryptocurrency businesses. Market participants must invest in robust compliance systems, conduct due diligence, and implement strong internal controls to meet regulatory obligations.

Heightened regulatory scrutiny may impact market entry for new cryptocurrency projects and startups. Regulatory barriers can limit innovation by imposing complex licensing processes, stifling competition, and deterring potential investors.

Enhanced investor protection measures can foster market confidence and attract institutional investors. More straightforward regulations on cryptocurrency offerings, custody services, and disclosures ensure that investors are adequately informed and protected against fraud and market manipulation.

Regulatory changes can influence market liquidity and trading volume. Stricter regulations may reduce speculative activities and illicit behavior, increasing market stability. However, more manageable regulations can drive trading volume to less regulated jurisdictions, potentially fragmenting the market.

Governments worldwide are developing taxation frameworks for cryptocurrencies. Clear guidelines on the taxation of cryptocurrency transactions, capital gains, and income tax obligations provide clarity for investors and promote tax compliance.

Regulatory changes related to cross-border transactions impact international remittances, cross-border trading, and the transfer of digital assets. Harmonized regulations and increased cooperation between jurisdictions are necessary to ensure seamless cross-border transactions.

Regulatory changes often introduce reporting obligations for cryptocurrency exchanges and service providers. Compliance with reporting requirements, such as transaction monitoring, suspicious activity reporting, and customer information sharing, enhances transparency and regulatory oversight.

Regulators increasingly establish sandboxes and regulatory experiments to facilitate innovation while maintaining oversight. These initiatives allow startups to test their ideas within a controlled environment, enabling regulators to assess the impact of new technologies and business models.

Collaboration between industry participants and regulators promotes dialogue, helps shape regulations, and ensures that regulatory changes consider the unique aspects of the cryptocurrency industry. Engaging with regulatory bodies allows for a balanced approach that fosters innovation while addressing concerns.

Self-regulatory organizations within the cryptocurrency industry, such as industry associations and code of conduct initiatives, can complement government regulations. These initiatives help establish industry standards, promote ethical practices, and enhance investor trust.

Emerging technologies and their influence on cryptocurrencies

The cryptocurrency industry continues to evolve rapidly, driven by technological advancements and innovative solutions. Emerging technologies can potentially revolutionize how cryptocurrencies are created, exchanged, and utilized. This section explores the influence of emerging technologies on cryptocurrencies, focusing on critical areas such as blockchain scalability, privacy-enhancing technologies, interoperability solutions, and decentralized applications. By examining these technologies, we gain insights into their potential to shape the future of digital assets and the broader implications for the cryptocurrency industry.

Emerging layer-two solutions, such as the Lightning Network and state channels, aim to enhance blockchain scalability by enabling off-chain transactions. These solutions reduce congestion on the main blockchain and increase transaction throughput, improving the efficiency and scalability of cryptocurrencies.

Sharding is an emerging technology that addresses scalability challenges by partitioning blockchain networks into smaller, interconnected shards. Each shard processes a portion of the network's transactions, enabling parallel processing and increasing the overall transaction capacity of the blockchain.

Sidechains are separate blockchain networks that are interoperable with the main blockchain. They allow for the execution of specific functions or applications without affecting the main blockchain's performance. Sidechains enable scalability by offloading certain transaction types or computations to secondary chains.

Zero-Knowledge Proofs (ZKPs) provide a way to verify the validity of information without revealing the actual data. ZKPs enable privacy-preserving transactions and allow users to prove ownership or knowledge of specific data without disclosing sensitive information. Technologies like zk-SNARKs and zk-STARKs offer robust privacy features for cryptocurrencies.

Confidential transactions employ cryptographic techniques to hide transaction amounts while ensuring transaction validity. By obfuscating the transaction amounts, confidentiality is enhanced, protecting the privacy of users and preventing transaction value leakage.

Privacy-focused cryptocurrencies like Monero and Zcash leverage advanced cryptographic techniques to provide anonymous and untraceable transactions. These cryptocurrencies use technologies like ring signatures, stealth addresses, and zero-knowledge proofs to maintain privacy and protect user identities.

Interoperability solutions aim to enable seamless communication and value transfer between different blockchain networks. Protocols like Polkadot, Cosmos, and interoperability-focused bridges facilitate interoperability by transferring assets across multiple blockchains, fostering collaboration and expanding the use cases of cryptocurrencies.

Atomic swaps enable peer-to-peer exchange of assets between different blockchain networks without the need for intermediaries. This technology allows for decentralized and trustless cross-chain transactions, enhancing liquidity and promoting efficient asset exchange.

Blockchain oracles provide external data to smart contracts, enabling them to interact with real-world events and off-chain data. Oracles play a crucial role in interoperability by facilitating cross-chain communication and enabling decentralized applications (dApps) to access information from external sources.

Smart contracts are self-executing contracts with the agreement's terms built directly into the code. They enable the creation of decentralized applications that operate on blockchain networks, providing transparency, immutability, and automated execution of predefined conditions.

Decentralized Finance (DeFi) applications leverage blockchain technology and smart contracts to recreate traditional financial systems in a decentralized manner. These applications offer lending, borrowing, decentralized exchanges, and yield farming features, providing users with increased financial autonomy and new opportunities for generating returns.

Non-Fungible Tokens (NFTs) are unique digital assets representing ownership or proof of authenticity for various types of digital and physical items. NFTs have gained popularity in areas such as digital art, collectibles, and virtual real estate, enabling new forms of ownership and monetization.

Emerging scalability solutions address the current limitations of blockchain networks, enabling faster and more efficient transactions. Improved scalability fosters broader adoption and usability of cryptocurrencies for payment and value transfer.

Privacy-enhancing technologies give users greater control over their personal information and transaction details. Enhanced privacy measures protect against surveillance, data leaks, and potential misuse of sensitive information, promoting user confidence in cryptocurrencies.

Interoperability solutions enable seamless interaction between different blockchain networks, facilitating the transfer of assets and data. Enhanced interoperability expands the utility of cryptocurrencies, enabling cross-chain asset transfers, decentralized exchanges, and the development of interconnected ecosystems.

Decentralized applications, particularly in the realms of finance and digital ownership, have the potential to disrupt traditional industries. DeFi applications challenge conventional financial intermediaries, while NFTs revolutionize the concept of digital ownership and intellectual property rights.

Long-term outlook for cryptocurrency investments

Cryptocurrencies have garnered significant attention in recent years, attracting investors from all walks of life. While the market is known for its volatility and short-term fluctuations, understanding the long-term outlook for cryptocurrency investments is essential for informed decision-making. This section explores the long-term prospects of cryptocurrency investments, examining key factors such as technological advancements, institutional adoption, regulatory developments, market maturation, and global adoption. We can better equip investors to handle the constantly changing world of digital assets by examining these aspects and gaining insights into future possibilities and problems that may arise.

Blockchain technology, the foundation of cryptocurrencies, continues to evolve and improve. Advancements in scalability, privacy, and interoperability solutions enhance the efficiency and usability of blockchain networks, increasing the long-term potential of cryptocurrencies.

Smart contracts enable the development of decentralized applications that operate on blockchain networks. The growth of dApps, particularly in decentralized finance (DeFi) and non-fungible tokens (NFTs), offers new opportunities for innovation and long-term value creation.

Layer-two solutions, like Lightning Network and sidechains, address scalability challenges by enabling off-chain transactions. These solutions enhance network capacity, transaction speed, and user experience, positioning cryptocurrencies for broader adoption in the long term.

More institutional investors are entering the Bitcoin industry, including hedge funds, asset managers, and businesses. Institutional adoption brings liquidity, stability, and professional expertise, signaling confidence in the long-term viability of cryptocurrencies as an asset class.

Regulatory frameworks are evolving to accommodate cryptocurrencies, providing clarity and fostering investor confidence. As regulatory clarity improves, institutional investors can navigate compliance requirements more efficiently, further bolstering long-term investment prospects.

Cryptocurrencies are gradually gaining acceptance in mainstream society. The integration of cryptocurrencies into payment systems, ecommerce platforms, and remittance services enhances their utility and paves the way for widespread adoption in the long term.

Regulatory measures aimed at investor protection, such as anti-money laundering (AML) and know-your-customer (KYC) requirements, foster market integrity and investor confidence. As regulations evolve, fraudulent activities decrease, making cryptocurrencies a more attractive long-term investment option.

Market infrastructure, including exchanges, custodial services, and trading platforms, is developing to accommodate growing demand. As infrastructure improves, liquidity deepens, trading volumes increase, and institutional-grade services become more accessible, creating a favorable environment for long-term investments.

The cryptocurrency market is gradually maturing, becoming less susceptible to extreme price volatility and speculative behavior. As the market matures, price stability and increased market efficiency create an environment conducive to long-term investment strategies.

Cryptocurrencies hold significant potential for adoption in emerging markets. In regions with limited access to traditional financial services, cryptocurrencies can provide a means of financial inclusion, empowering individuals and businesses to participate in the global economy in the long term.

Some view cryptocurrencies as a hedge against traditional financial systems during economic uncertainty. In the long term, as economic conditions fluctuate, cryptocurrencies may offer an alternative store of value and a potential hedge against inflation.

The development of central bank digital currencies presents opportunities and challenges for cryptocurrencies. Central Bank Digital Currencies (CBDCs) may contribute to increased adoption and acceptance of digital assets in the long term while introducing new regulatory considerations and competition.

Cryptocurrencies are known for their volatility, which poses risks for long-term investors. Managing price fluctuations and emotional biases is crucial for maintaining a long-term investment strategy and mitigating potential risks.

While regulatory frameworks are evolving, regulatory uncertainty remains a challenge. Shifting regulations and compliance requirements can impact cryptocurrencies' long-term viability and growth, requiring investors to stay informed and adaptable.

Cryptocurrencies are built on complex technological foundations. Vulnerabilities, such as security breaches and software bugs, pose risks to cryptocurrencies' long-term stability and trustworthiness. Ongoing technological developments and robust security measures are vital to address these risks.

CONCLUSION

Recap of key points discussed in the e-book

Throughout this e-book, we have delved into various aspects of cryptocurrency investing, exploring topics ranging from the definition and characteristics of cryptocurrencies to technical analysis tools, risk management techniques, and emerging trends in the industry. In this section, we recap the key points discussed in the e-book, highlighting the essential takeaways for readers. By summarizing the main concepts, strategies, and considerations, we aim to provide a comprehensive overview that helps investors navigate the complex world of cryptocurrency investing with confidence and informed decision-making.

I.   Understanding Cryptocurrencies

- Cryptocurrencies are digital assets that utilize cryptographic techniques to safeguard transactions, control the creation of new units, and enable decentralized peer-to-peer transactions.

- Key characteristics of cryptocurrencies include decentralization, transparency, immutability, and limited supply, distinguishing them from traditional fiat currencies.

- Bitcoin, the first and most well-known cryptocurrency, paved the way for thousands of alternative cryptocurrencies, each with unique features and use cases.

II. Investment Considerations

- Conduct thorough research prior investing in any cryptocurrency, considering factors such as technology, team, market demand, and potential risks.

- Understand the risks associated with cryptocurrency investing, including market volatility, regulatory uncertainty, security vulnerabilities, and technological risks.

- Define your investment goals and risk tolerance to develop a tailored investment strategy that aligns with your financial objectives.

III. Fundamental Analysis

- Evaluate the team and project behind a cryptocurrency, assessing their expertise, track record, and the project's use case viability.

- Read and interpret whitepapers and technical documentation to gain insights into a cryptocurrency's underlying technology, roadmap. and potential value proposition.

- Assess market demand and adoption potential by analyzing factors such as user adoption, partnerships, and real-world applications.

IV. Technical Analysis

- Use technical analysis tools and indicators to analyze price trends, identify support and resistance levels, and make informed investment decisions.

- Read and interpret cryptocurrency charts, including line, bar, and candlestick charts, to gain insights into historical price movements and patterns.

- Identify trends, support, and resistance levels to determine potential entry and exit points for investment.

V. Risk Management and Portfolio Diversification

- Implement risk management techniques such as setting stop-loss orders, diversifying your portfolio, and allocating investments based on risk tolerance and investment objectives.

- Understand the importance of dollar-cost averaging and other investment strategies to reduce the impact of market fluctuations and volatility.

- Stay updated with market news and trends, conduct thorough research, and make informed decisions to navigate the cryptocurrency market successfully.

VI. Market Outlook and Long-Term Considerations

- Consider the long-term outlook for cryptocurrency investments, considering technological advancements, institutional adoption, regulatory developments, and global acceptance.

- Recognize the possibility of emerging technologies, such as scalability solutions, privacy-enhancing technologies, and decentralized applications, to shape the future of digital assets.

- Understand the implications of regulatory changes on the cryptocurrency industry, including compliance requirements, taxation, and market infrastructure development.

In this comprehensive guide to cryptocurrency investing, we have covered various aspects of the industry, providing readers with valuable insights and strategies to navigate the dynamic world of digital assets. From understanding the fundamentals of cryptocurrencies to conducting thorough research, employing technical analysis tools, managing risks, and considering long-term prospects, investors have gained a holistic understanding of the critical factors that drive success in cryptocurrency investing.

Recognizing that the cryptocurrency market is continuously evolving is crucial, and staying informed and adaptable is essential for sustained success. As you embark on your cryptocurrency investment journey, continue to educate yourself, monitor market trends, and refine your strategies. By employing sound investment principles, embracing technological advancements, and remaining vigilant, you can position yourself to maximize the potential of cryptocurrency investments in the years to come.

Remember, investing in cryptocurrencies involves risks, and it is always prudent to seek professional advice and conduct thorough due diligence prior making any investment decisions. With the proper knowledge, research, and a disciplined approach, you can confidently navigate the cryptocurrency landscape and capitalize on the opportunities presented by this transformative asset class.

Final thoughts on the potential of cryptocurrencies

As we conclude this comprehensive exploration of cryptocurrencies, it is essential to reflect on the remarkable potential and transformative power that these digital assets hold. Throughout this e-book, we have examined the various facets of cryptocurrencies, including their definition, characteristics, investment strategies, technological advancements, and market trends. In this section, we offer final thoughts on the potential of cryptocurrencies, highlighting their impact on finance, society, and the global economy. We discuss the potential benefits, challenges, and implications of this digital revolution, ultimately painting a picture of a future where cryptocurrencies play a pivotal role in shaping our financial systems and empowering individuals worldwide.

I.   Advancing Financial Inclusion and Empowerment

Cryptocurrencies can potentially eliminate barriers and provide access to financial services for the unbanked and also underbanked populations. By leveraging mobile technology and the internet, cryptocurrencies can empower individuals in developing countries, fostering economic growth and reducing the wealth gap.

Cryptocurrencies enable peer-to-peer transactions without the need for intermediaries, offering fast, secure, and low-cost cross-border payment solutions. This could revolutionize remittance services, international trade, and financial interactions, promoting economic efficiency and global connectivity.

Cryptocurrencies empower individuals to take control of their financial lives by giving them ownership and control over their digital assets. With enhanced privacy features, individuals can transact securely, free from excessive surveillance and the prying eyes of centralized institutions.

II. Disrupting Traditional Financial Systems

Decentralized Finance (DeFi) applications, built on blockchain technology, challenge traditional financial intermediaries by providing transparent, secure, and efficient financial services. With decentralized lending, borrowing, and asset management platforms, individuals can access financial services without relying on banks or other traditional institutions.

Cryptocurrencies enable the tokenization of real-world assets, such as real estate, artwork, and intellectual property. This digital representation of physical assets opens up new avenues for ownership, fractional investment, and global liquidity, democratizing access to traditionally illiquid markets.

Smart contracts, powered by blockchain technology, automate the execution of predefined agreements without the need for intermediaries. This can streamline complex processes, reduce costs, and enhance transparency and trust in various sectors, such as supply chain management, insurance, and legal services.

III. Technological Advancements and Innovation

Scalability solutions, such as layer-two protocols and sharding, are poised to address the scalability challenges faced by blockchain networks, enabling higher transaction throughput and improved user experience. This paves the way for the mass adoption of cryptocurrencies and the development of scalable decentralized applications.

Interoperability solutions facilitate seamless communication and value transfer between different blockchain networks, fostering collaboration and expanding the use cases of cryptocurrencies. This interoperability can unlock the full potential of decentralized finance, asset tokenization, and cross-chain applications.

Cryptocurrencies are evolving to address privacy concerns and enhance security measures. Innovations such as zero-knowledge proofs, confidential transactions, and privacy-focused cryptocurrencies offer individuals greater control over their personal data, transactions, and digital identities.

IV. Regulatory Considerations and Market Maturity

Regulatory developments are crucial for the widespread adoption and acceptance of cryptocurrencies. Striking a balance between innovation and investor protection, regulatory frameworks provide clarity, mitigate risks, and foster institutional participation in the cryptocurrency market.

As the cryptocurrency market matures, institutional investors are increasingly entering the space, bringing professional expertise, liquidity, and stability. This institutional adoption signals growing confidence in cryptocurrencies as a legitimate asset class and encourages broader adoption and acceptance.

Cryptocurrencies are gaining acceptance worldwide, with governments, central banks, and multinational corporations exploring the potential of digital currencies and blockchain technology. This global integration contributes to the normalization of cryptocurrencies and their integration into existing financial systems.

V. Embracing the Future

The potential of cryptocurrencies has yet to fully realize. Ongoing innovation, technological advancements, and new use cases will keep on shaping the future of digital assets. Remaining open-minded and adaptable is key to capturing the opportunities this ever-evolving landscape presents.

As with any investment, responsible investing and risk management are paramount. Educate yourself, diversify your portfolio, set realistic expectations, and approach cryptocurrency investing with a long-term mindset. This approach allows you to navigate the volatility and fluctuations while capitalizing on the potential growth of digital assets.

Education and community engagement are essential to harness the potential of cryptocurrencies fully. Stay informed, participate in discussions, attend conferences, and collaborate with like-minded individuals to share knowledge and contribute to the development of this transformative industry.

Cryptocurrencies can reshape our financial systems, foster inclusivity, and empower individuals worldwide. By democratizing access to financial services, disrupting traditional intermediaries, and embracing technological advancements, cryptocurrencies unlock new possibilities for financial sovereignty, economic growth, and global connectivity.

As we move forward, it is essential to recognize this digital revolution's potential benefits and challenges. With responsible investing, a commitment to ongoing education, and a proactive approach to risk management, we can navigate the evolving landscape of cryptocurrencies and capitalize on their transformative potential.

Embrace the future of finance, participate actively in the cryptocurrency ecosystem, and contribute to the ongoing revolution that will shape how we perceive, interact with, and benefit from financial systems. Together, let us unlock the immense potential of cryptocurrencies and build a more inclusive, transparent, and empowered financial future for all.